in Germany.
My story.

Ne pas choisir, c'est encore choisir...

Oh, my love, my darling,
I hate you when you're drunk...
You morph, so quickly
Into that irresponsible punk...
You were my type,
When we were young.
But now we're getting old,
So please, wake up!

I want a baby
so bad 4

The 'normal'
birth experience 45

The C-section
birth Experience 102

Personal guidance
for you 132

I want a baby so bad.

When moving around the world, it can be difficult to feel at home. Try to resist the urge to compare the new place to the previous ones, and lower your expectations so you don't get disappointed too often. There will always be pros and cons to consider, but learn to make the most of it, no matter where you end up living.

(_/)
(• . •)
(.) (.)
❀✿❁❃❂❋

The 1st of March... the beginning of a colorful spring with flowers everywhere. Birds are chirping happily, the skies are blue, and the sun is shining. It's one of those perfect days, warm but not too hot, the kind where you want to hang out with friends in nature, breathe the fresh air, and feel the gentle breeze touching your cheeks.

'It's the perfect season for a big change!' we concur without hesitation.

After giving a lot of thought to the idea of leaving our home country for a 'better' one, my husband and I decide to move abroad and start a new life there. Most of our friends are either leaving the country as well, or buying properties and making family plans. Time is flying so fast and it just feels like we need to do something new, to start over in a new place.

Germany was never on our destinations list, but since the best job offer my husband gets is there, we agree to give it a shot. Now, when I think about it, it wasn't the best idea... but we live and we learn from our mistakes rather than repeat them, this is what makes us human. We come from an eastern European country, so forgive us for thinking: 'the German system will offer us a better quality of life'. Four days after the International Women's Day we arrive at our temporary accommodation in a nice smallish university city, situated halfway between Stuttgart and Munich, in south Germany. Let's call it Schwabendream, since locals use the Schwäbisch dialect as their primary communication tool.

Our first year in Deutschland is a very enjoyable one, just like a long, relaxing, holiday. We are young and in love, and moving to a new place, and adapting to the new environment is really exciting for both of us. It's true that the weather is not always on our side, considering the long rainy season and the almost permanent fog, but the geographical position of the city is awesome, and it gives us the opportunity to travel around Europe without having to spend endless hours on the road. Only fifty minutes' drive to the stunning Alps and a couple of breathtaking lakes, four hours by train to Paris and six hours to Venice, plus some of the nicest thermal baths in Germany are located just around the corner.

Everything is new – the country, the city, the language. And believe me when I say it, learning German is mandatory if you want to be able to successfully integrate into the local community. It's an essential skill that helps you fit in. If you wish to have a 'normal' life, to make friends and maybe start a family in Germany, knowing the language might come in very handy. On the other hand, not being able to speak it can make your life miserable. You will most likely end up feeling alone and unwanted, and you will probably give up and move away after one year, or less. Language can be a real barrier in Germany, I'm not joking! Ask my husband. He wasn't able to learn it in seven years... Not my case, as I always enjoy a linguistic challenge. However, in the beginning, my only contact with this 'brutal' language was music. Not classical, but Rammstein, one of the few German bands who managed to break outside of the local scene and masterfully create something so unique that even people who aren't fluent in German love their fabulous industrial songs, videos and live-shows. If you don't know them yet, it's time to do your research. 'Du riechst so gut' is one of my favorite songs ever.

It took me one full year to be able to speak German at an intermediate level, one year of daily struggle with this very non-artistic language. Five years later, I managed to get my C1 certificate in German, after six months of intensive self-study. I decided to skip B2 level since, after living for a couple of years in Germany, I am already able to understand almost everything, and I can keep up with a complex conversation between native speakers in real time.

To be completely honest, I've always felt that German is the best language for yelling at someone, if you want to scare the heck out of them. So mastering it can be a useful skill.

Let's do an exercise. Stand in front of a mirror and say out loud:

Heilige Scheiße! (*ei* pronounced /ai/ as in 'eye', *sch* /sh/ as in 'sheet', *ß* exactly like the /s/ sound)

Halt die Klappe, du Arschloch! (*ie* /ee/ as in 'beer', *sch* /sh/ as in 'sheet')

Du blöder Waschlappen! (*ö* pronounced like the /i/ in 'bird', *sch* /sh/ as in 'sheet')

How do these words make you feel?

✳✳✳✳

Later in June, we manage to rent a small furnished apartment in the city center, and we start looking for human contact in the cafés nearby. Our initial attempts to make German friends are not really successful. To our disappointment, the vast majority of local people are acting friendly in a very fake way. They smile occasionally, and engage in polite conversations, answer questions, and offer information. They are great at having a meaningful and honest chat. And that's about it. If you are used to making small talk, and hang out around the coffee machine with no specific purpose, you are going to be disappointed. German people already have their friends and families. Why should they become friends with you?! Nevertheless, not all of them are cold and unwelcoming. If you try hard enough, you might get the chance to meet some Germans who will be happy to practice their English skills with you, and even reveal some hidden secrets about the turbulent history behind Germany's most iconic castles, while enjoying a giant pretzel smeared with Obazda and a Maß of Hefeweizen (1L of unfiltered wheat beer). Obazda is a delicious Bavarian cheese-mix that you can enjoy in beer gardens. It's also available in stores but you can also easily prepare it at home. You'll need:

200g Camembert (mashed)
100g cream cheese
20g butter
a half of a medium onion – finely chopped
salt and pepper
optional: paprika powder and fresh parsley.
Mix all the ingredients in a bowl.
Enjoy!

❋❋❋❋

There are more women than men in Germany, and despite the narrowing of the gender wage gap in recent years, they still get paid less compared to their male colleagues. However, in my opinion, German women are very strong, both physically and psychically, very independent and self-confident, maybe because they don't care so much about looks and clothing. For them, it's all about comfort, about being practical, not about being fancy and stylish. You won't normally see a lot of elegant ladies on the streets of Germany. And I loved that aspect of living in Deutschland because it allowed me to relax, and just enjoy the freedom of wearing jeans and sneakers on a daily basis. The German uncomplicated, and very functional dress code, spared me a lot of time and money, and honestly, it feels less frustrating to have a simple wardrobe.

German men, on the other hand, seem to be really shy and passive. They hate confrontation of any sort (the 'no-balls' type of guys). And even if they are highly educated and manage to achieve good job positions, their mental weakness, and their lack of masculine strength, gave me the impression of resilience, mediocrity and ignorance.

Nevertheless, there is one place where you will see German balls walking around: **the gym**. German people really enjoy their Freikörperkultur (free body culture/nudity) inside, and out in nature, in their gardens, in public parks, along the coastline, in the sauna, or in the gym. (Beware: German saunas are mixed-gender and clothing-free!)

In the locker room, they will shake your hand and tell you 'funny' stories while drying their pubic hair. Even shaving your intimate area in the gym shower is not an issue in Deutschland, so don't feel weird if you notice some packages on display. No one really considers these things too suggestive, or personal. Nail clipping and/or nose hair trimming is also common, so try not to be shocked if you see someone doing it.

Another 'good to know' fact about Germans is that they love dogs more than children. In some cases, landlords prefer dogs to kids because kids usually make a lot of noise and they tend to attract even more kids, and that can disturb the neighbors. It can be difficult, and very expensive, to rent an apartment if you are bringing your kids to Germany.

My brother and I grew up with our beloved dog, and best friend, Noir. He was always there when we needed him, watching us with his huge beautiful brown eyes. He was ours to take care of, and he made us smile every day. He listened to us without being judgmental, he understood us in a way no human being could. Although I am not currently a dog owner, I do love dogs. But I have to admit that there are certain breeds I'm afraid of, especially since I became a mother. Dogs and kids can get along great but they can also get into all kinds of trouble if unsupervised.

In Germany the majority of dog owners don't keep their dogs on a leash, and it can get really dangerous if you have impulsive, fearless, and exuberant kids like mine. Still, if you ask me, the problem with these 'dangerous' dogs is their irresponsible owners, who need to wake up and understand that a dog, just like any other animal, might get anxious, worried or agitated, and he might feel the need to bite. Dear German dog owners, please, start using leashes and/or muzzles in public areas. Let's live together in peace and happiness. This world is big enough, for both families with young kids, and families with dogs, so let's start respecting each other more!

✼✼✼✼

In 99% of the families we meet in Germany, mothers are totally relaxed about everything concerning their kids. They are my complete opposite... and no matter how much I try to 'steal' some of their calm, I just can't stop being that overprotective mom, who spends all her free time and energy on raising the kids. And since my fear of doctors plays a big role in my life, I usually manage to see only the unsafe and the unpredictable part of this crazy world we are living in.

Generally speaking, parenting 'the German way' means motivating your little ones towards positive behavior by giving them plenty of space. Encouraging them to explore their potential by getting wet and dirty, by eating sand, by playing with dangerous items like bike tool kits and knives, and ignoring bad behavior by simply walking away (for example when your kid decides to throw a tantrum) are highly practiced behaviors.

Most of the German married couples we meet while living in Germany, prefer living close to their parents/in-laws. By doing so, after having kids, they are able to get help with different 'small' things like taking the children to/from school, or driving them around to their various activities and sports. They also enjoy family meals and celebrate birthday parties together, allowing their kids to receive endless love and attention from their grandparents. However, they never move in with them because they know that having your family around full-time could cause a lot of problems and frustration for everybody.

So yeah, raising children near your parents has a lot of mutual benefits, besides the babysitting and the free food, and German families seem to understand that very well. Maybe that's also one of the reasons why German moms manage to merge motherhood so easily into their identity. This is something completely new for me, since in my family, 'the mother' was that poor woman drowning in stress, the one who received no help whatsoever from her family, and always worried about the safety of her children. Organizing our life, cooking our meals, taking care of us when we were sick, that was my mother's daily routine, when she was not in the office. My father was never really involved in our lives. And it's not just his case. All the fathers I knew in my childhood smoked cigarettes and were a sort of extra feature when it came to raising kids.

Until we've reached age seven, my brother and I were spending nine hours every day in a kindergarten. After 4pm, our mother was the one picking us up, and hanging out with us. Our father used to come home only late in the evening, and sometimes even decided to spend the night away, especially after a marital fight. But, in spite of that, he's the one who taught us to respect nature, and every living creature, to play chess, and listen to good music. He also encouraged us to be creative in whatever we did. Well, I guess he did his best, considering that he and mom never got along...

In my husband's family the situation looks a bit different. Women cook, do the dishes, clean the house, but they also criticize a lot, and (usually) have the final say. My husband and his brother were practically raised by their grandparents. Even now, they don't use the words 'mom' and 'dad' with their parents, and one of their grandmothers still cooks for the whole family on a daily basis. Sometimes it feels like there is a lot of tension between his mother and his two grand-mothers. They judge each other constantly but they've somehow learned to tolerate one another's crap. Nothing and no one is good enough for them, and they think they know everything. That's the reason we don't visit them too often, especially after having kids of our own.

As parents, my husband and I invest much more time into raising our children because we are able to do so. We are involved with them day and night, we talk about everything, we play together, we watch cartoons and anime, and we do far more for them than our parents did for us (sometimes maybe too much).

I strongly believe that I'm the backbone of this family. My husband does help me when he can, but I always have to make very specific requests if I want the job done right because he's somehow unable to 'feel' our family's needs. Nevertheless, he's the one working a full-time job, which takes a lot of time and energy, so he does have an excuse, I suppose.

Having had the opportunity to embrace the crazy adventure of pregnancy and birth (twice) helped me transform into a more mature person, and definitely into a helicopter-mom. It all started the day our one year old daughter decided to go out of our apartment on her own, and fell down an entire flight of stairs. I felt so guilty and ashamed for not being able to protect her, so I promised myself I would do everything I can to keep something like that from happening again.

Preventable accidents? No thank you, not when I'm around. Helicopter mode: ACTIVATED.

Because of my fear of doctors I tend to take care of my kids in a way some people would characterize as helicopter-parenting. But you know what, it doesn't actually bother me. Especially when it comes from childless people, or parents who constantly fail to protect their own children. Hovering over my kids might make playtime less enjoyable sometimes, but it also keeps everyone safer. As much as parents love and trust their offspring, the truth is that some accidents could be easily avoided if adults would take more precautions.

I like to think of myself as a normal mom, who juggles everyday life challenges with two small children. I don't smoke – I used to, but gave up more than ten years ago, I only drink occasionally, and I really enjoy home cooked meals prepared with healthy ingredients, and lots of love. I like being protective and vigilant, that's why I avoid dangerous activities, and I try to reduce the chances of having an accident to a minimum. My life is cool as it is, as long as I don't have to see a doctor.

Nevertheless, I have to admit that I'm an anxious mom, not a trustful one. There are occasions when I would like to allow my children to explore this world in freedom, but my fears always stop me from doing that. My life as a helicopter mom is not easy but, let's be honest about one thing, there are real dangers out there! Pedophiles, dogs without leashes, and cars, are just a few of them. I know my fears are most of the time exaggerated most of the time, but they're based on real-life situations.

Finding a balance between fear and joy, transcending my anxiety (that sometimes ruins our family's cheerful moments), protecting my kids but also enjoying life, those are some of the issues I'm struggling with so often. Still, I'm looking forward to growing my knowledge and skills as a mom, and I know I'm doing the best I can. In my opinion, having kids is a permanent and radical change in one's life. You can either love it or hate it. It's your choice and you shouldn't underestimate the impact a tiny human being will have on your existence. Parenting is for sure one of the hardest jobs in the world. It's like being 'on call' every day, while trying to act like a grown-up, even when you are completely terrified. The continuous state of exhaustion and self-sacrifice, the huge responsibility, the extreme tantrums that you cannot temper even if you read a ton of books and blogs about it, those are some facts a non-parent would never truly understand.

Dear people without kids, I almost no longer remember how easy my life was when I was like you... You don't have kids, and you don't really know anything about MY kids. It would be great if you could stop giving me advice on how to raise them. They certainly are the center of my universe, they influence my eating habits, my behavior, and my life, but you won't be able to understand that until you've experienced it yourself. Remaining childfree is a conscious decision, just like my decision to have kids. We don't have to be friends. We live in totally different worlds, but we should do the best we can to tolerate each other.

❊❊❊❊

During our first year in Germany, Schwabendream, the medium sized city located on the Danube River, was a very clean and beautiful place to live in. The charming old town with its Gothic church, and its well preserved walls, the picturesque houses, and the narrow alleys and bridges, made a very nice area to explore by day or by night. The city and its surroundings offered their guests a variety of shopping and dining opportunities, and all kinds of leisure activities. We loved the nice bio-stores selling affordable, but high quality products, the Drogerien, where you can find everything except for fresh food and clothes, and we really appreciated the German supermarket-chains, which are very well organized, compared to the huge French-style hypermarkets where we used to grocery shop before moving to Germany.

As newcomers in town, we were lucky enough to get to know a bunch of very interesting and funny people who, just like us, decided to try the 'German adventure' and moved to Schwabendream. We went out together at least twice a week, trying out different types of local food, and drinking all sorts of German beer.

Nowadays, the city has changed a lot, and not for the better. The interesting people moved away, or decided against having kids, a huge number of immigrants came to Deutschland, some of them refusing to make the effort to learn the language, adopt the local lifestyle, and integrate quickly. Schwabendream has become a crowded and dirty place, full of young men seeking jobs.

I do believe that sometimes non-integrating immigration can harm, or even abuse, the native cultures. And the sad reality is that most German people are racist, whether they are aware of it, or not.

If your parents are not Deutsche, or if you speak with an accent, you will feel discriminated against at some point, maybe as a patient in a hospital, or as a candidate searching for a new job.

South Germany might be a nice place to live in, but to be completely honest, we never felt fully accepted as German citizens because the Bundesstaat as a whole is a racist country, just like many other European countries. And even if they are trying to become more open and tolerant, an 'Ausländer' will forever be an 'Ausländer' in the eyes of local people.

After living several years in Schwabendream, we gradually start feeling the urge to leave Deutschland permanently, so we decide to switch jobs and continue our European journey somewhere else. We end up in Fancytopia, a bigger and more cosmopolitan city, nestled between Germany, France and Belgium.

Compared to Schwabendream, our new home city has three official languages and, because half of its residents are expats, almost everyone can also speak English. It is one of the most expensive cities for rental properties in Europe. The average prices are unbelievably high, but the quality of what you get for the money you pay is either lower or, at best, the same as what we used to have in Germany. Everything is a little 'French': louder, dirtier, and fancier. And the odds of getting head-lice if you have kids are very big, just like in France. The one time in my adult life when I managed to get them was while working as a babysitter in Paris. In Deutschland, even after having kids, head-lice were never a problem.

Since we just moved here, it would be unfair to already categorize this city. But, I can't resist the urge to criticize the lack of an efficient public transportation system, which, even if free for everyone to use, didn't manage to resolve one of the major issues that suffocate this city – traffic jams. Fancytopia's residents are typically stylish and busy people, who are always driving somewhere. Imagine those elegant ladies wearing high heels and chic dresses having to walk to the office, or those fancy guys with their classical French hairstyles, having to wear a beanie in winter. Nope. Not possible! Their big, shiny, and warm car is their number one friend. So, if you hate cars like I do (what am I doing here?!), this place is not for you.

Besides the local drivers, there are around 200.000 people who commute into Fancytopia five days a week. All this come-and-go contributes to the eternal traffic congestion that paralyzes the city, and poisons the air. Sometimes, I don't feel like opening the windows because of the smog hanging in the sky.

Being the capital of one of the smallest and richest countries in the world might give one the impression that Fancytopia possesses enough financial resources to invest more extensively in environmental measures. The truth is that the local council doesn't care at all about air pollution, and they failed to take action against the main air polluting source, the nitrogen oxides produced by vehicle fuel combustion.

However, as someone said before, a city succeeds when people want to live, work, and spend their money there. And the majority of Fancytopia's residents aren't bothered by the poor air quality in their city, so the situation will probably get worse before it starts getting better.

A lot of people see this place as a temporary destination because of the high level of salaries and bonuses. They spend a couple of years here and leave after they've saved enough money, either because of the lack of community cohesion, or simply because they hate the climate, the heavy rain and strong winds that can bring melancholy and negative vibes with them. Sadly, Fancytopia is somehow unable to seduce its fellow expats citizens, get closer to them, and convince them to stay, even if overall it's a more enjoyable place to live in than most of the other European countries we've lived in.

Compared to Schwabendream, Fancytopia's educational system seems to be more efficient and complex. But the lack of free places in state-run childcare institutions gives me the impression that this country doesn't really want to help expat moms settle in. And the vast majority of them actually don't.

If you want to be able to have a job, you have to put your kids in a private Crèche or Foyer, and it can get really expensive because they will charge you for 60 hours/week even if your kid spends less time there. Anyhow, all the mothers I meet here enjoy having an office to go to everyday, even when that's not a real financial necessity for them.

Mandatory school starts when your child turns four. Kids are really learning stuff, and they enjoy having to work on different tasks and projects every day. But, there is something totally unacceptable that makes me very angry every time it occurs. For some weird reason, kids eat a lot of sweets inside childcare facilities, babies included...

When I ask the lady from the Crèche, why they offer candy to the kids, she throws me a stupidly naïve but sincere answer: 'They are kids, they are happy when they receive sweets, so we are just trying to keep them happy. And they brush their teeth after every meal!'

Back in Schwabendream, we used to be bothered by the fact that small kids were treated like animals in kindergarten. They played a lot by themselves, got really dirty every single day, and were constantly sick. One rainy day, I picked up our daughter around 3 o'clock in the afternoon, and she was really, really dirty, full of mud everywhere, even in her underwear. I asked her what she did to look like that, and her answer was 'I wanted to play with Frau Klein but she told me I should better go outside, and dig a big hole. So today I dug a very big hole!' And it was huge, and full of muddy water, a five year old could easily fit inside.

I know, I know, kids need to feel free, to enjoy nature, and mud and sand, and all the dirty natural things. But let's face it, it's not like we adults go outside when it's really cold and windy, so why should our kids stay out in the rain, get wet and freeze? (especially if they don't want to...) Many Germans say 'There is no bad weather, only bad clothing', but maybe, just maybe, not all of us were born to freeze!

Our daughter told us she sometimes didn't want to play in the garden, but she had to, together with all her peers. Furthermore, it was during kindergarten, in Schwabendream, when she learned a mild version of bullying, which was not condemned by teachers at all, but tacitly accepted instead. She also started spitting and using bad expressions when she got angry: something like 'I hate you, you should die!' One of the teachers was laughing at me, when I mentioned it to her, saying that it was a pretty normal and funny thing for the kids to do. On top of that, the fact that our daughter was not able to speak German to her peers was a big minus for us. That happened mainly because when a child started talking or singing in her/his mother tongue, the teachers didn't stop her/him. Only a few kids could actually speak German, and no one really helped them improve their language skills by making the use of German mandatory. But again, what to expect from those kids when their parents, who were born and raised in Germany, weren't able to speak proper German?!

❃❃❃❃

Now, going back to the beginning of our journey in Deutschland, the country of beer, sausages and social assistance, let me tell you how we've managed to conceive and raise two wonderful, and very agitated kids, in a place where peaceful multiculturalism is still a work in progress. As we all know, getting fluent in a foreign language is usually a big commitment. Motivation plays an important role and could determine how quickly one can learn a language. I am aware that learning German would take a significant amount of time and effort from my side, but after successfully finishing a language course, I am convinced that even with my basic B1 level I will be able to get a new job.

As it turns out, finding a good job in Schwabendream, without a proper dose of vitamin B, is impossible. German employers are very careful when it comes to hiring a young married woman. They will always ask the baby question, and even if you don't want kids, the chances that they will actually believe you are very low. Besides that, if you are not German and you don't have any 'Beziehungen' (connections), it might be extremely complicated to pass an interview, and secure an offer.

After trying several 'mini-jobs', I am forced to accept that it might take longer than expected to reach my career goals in Deutschland.

Meanwhile, all of a sudden, my brain gets really hit by the 'I want a baby, and I want it NOW!' crazy hormones. I've always asked myself where this hormonal storm came from, what its purpose was, and why I was not able to control it. 'IT' has been quietly infiltrating my mind for some time, tricking it into believing that the perfect moment to start a family has arrived. Everyone is asking me about my future babies, our grandparents, our parents, aunts and uncles, friends, teachers, and even random people, like doctors.

Many of my female friends are already expecting their first child. I start seeing pregnant ladies everywhere, and I wonder how it feels to be pregnant. Those weird hormones keep raging wildly through my system, and they eventually manage to take control over my mental faculties. I quickly decide I must have a baby in the next months.

Now, I'm not saying I didn't want to have kids, but I'm not sure anymore whether it was my idea, or maybe I just felt trapped by the social pressure that our families, friends, and acquaintances exerted upon us. If I would be given the chance to start the parenting adventure all over again, I would do more research about the crappy parts of motherhood. Why?, you might ask. It's because having lived my life as a relaxed young adult female with a lot of spare time on my hands made me see only the positive aspects of having a baby, and I was really naïve believing that I could control everything.

They say one is never 100% ready to have a baby, but it doesn't mean you can't be 80% ready, or at least 60%... My husband and I were probably 20% ready when I gave birth to our daughter. Of course, we somehow managed to adapt to the situation, but the birth experience, and the first months that followed it, were hell on earth, especially for me.

Lucky for you, you can learn from my mistakes. Here's what you should consider if you are starting to think about getting pregnant.

1. Ask your mother/sister/aunt/female friend who has kids about her real

experiences as a mom. Don't be afraid to hear the bad side of the story because that's actually the important side. Let's be realistic, no one has a pain free life! We all wish to be happy and try to ignore the negative parts of our existence, but we all suffer, and we all struggle sometimes, and it's absolutely ok. You should inform yourself properly, from reliable sources, before going through conception, childbirth, and motherhood.

2. Make sure your partner wants to be a parent too because if they don't, you'll end up raising your kids all by yourself! Some people remain mentally and/or emotionally immature their entire life, even after having children. And, although all mothers think that their babies are the most adorable creatures on this planet, only few people are willing to admit that having a baby ruined their relationship. Actually, most couples start having problems after the birth of their second child because that's the moment when the partner must step up, and has to accept the

fact that they won't get any breaks from their kids anymore. With two kids, everything requires more organization, and parents barely have time for anything. So try to accept your life as it is, and, despite the fact that you feel you don't love your partner anymore (or even hate them), give your relationship another chance. It will get better after a couple of years, so be patient.

3. Be aware that being a parent means making a lot of compromises, and it can bring a lot of guilt into your life. The lack of sleep, the responsibilities that come along with your newborn, the wave of feelings that hits you when your baby cries and screams around the clock, those are just a few things that might transform your love life in a countless series of fights with your partner. But don't worry, you will eventually learn to lower your expectations, you'll probably start communicating once again, and you'll somehow manage to grow together as parents.

4. Even though you think your partner is 'the one', your soul-mate, your 'one and only', and even if you are extremely happy before having kids, please, keep in mind that you won't be the same lovey-dovey couple after having kids. Being a parent sucks a lot in the beginning!

5. Dear future parents, who are constantly imagining that your future progenies will be the most sensationally well behaved kids on Earth, and that they will do everything you expect them to do, when you say it and how you say it, you people who secretly hope that your life won't suffer any changes after having kids... to you guys, I can only say: Wake up! And good luck! You will definitely need it.

I have to laugh now when I think about how naïve I used to be before having kids. I remember talking to my fellow pregnant mommies during the prenatal classes. They were all very amused when I told them that I was planning on keeping my life as it was. I really believed that my baby would adapt to my lifestyle. Stupid, isn't it?! But true... I even said I would go to as many concerts as possible as soon as I'm out of the delivery room. And guess what, it didn't happen! Zero concerts. None... I still love my music, but after stepping into motherhood, I was always too tired, too paranoid, and too scared, to let anyone else take care of my babies.

As a new mom you can only dream about going out and party till sunrise, enjoy a hangover, wake up at noon, and stay in bed the rest of the day. Unless you have a full time nanny, or parents living near you, spending one week in an all-inclusive Kinderhotel with babysitting services will probably be your only chance to enjoy a relaxing getaway.

6. Make babies later in life, after you've had enough freedom! Enter parenthood only after you've been able to survive one month on self-cooked food. No takeaway meals, and no alcohol!

✷✷✷✷

Later in October, when many stores begin celebrating the Christmas season (from the moment Halloween is over), I start discussing and negotiating 'the baby dream' with my husband.

After a few days of analyzing, reviewing, and assessing our situation, we begin having a lot of wild unprotected sex, waiting for the miracle to happen. It takes me around five months to get pregnant, but it feels like an eternity.

For no real reason, I was living under the impression that I could not conceive a child, so the news of being pregnant surprises the crap out of me instead of bringing excitement and tears of joy into my eyes. My husband is totally freaked out, and shocked about the real possibility of having a baby, so he can't actually be happy about my pregnancy, even if he is really enjoying the wild unprotected sex. That is definitely the moment I start hating him... And, because of him being so insecure and overwhelmed by the situation, I start feeling guilty about being pregnant, and I don't let anybody know about the baby during the first four months.

I'm an ordinary person with an ordinary life, but I'm lucky enough to stay fit and healthy even if I don't do diets, or exercise regularly. I am 1.73m tall, and my normal weight is 58kg. Nevertheless, during the first months of pregnancy I begin losing weight, as I am confronted with a big problem: the everlasting nausea. I throw up only a couple of times, but I'm feeling nauseous constantly, and that's so annoying. I don't have much of an appetite. I am able to eat only bread and olives, and drink only milk. My body desperately craves milk. I'm constantly holding a bottle of milk in my hand. I am extremely tired, and feel the need to lie down pretty much all the time, but I'm unable to actually sleep.

Later on, when I am finally able to eat normally, I am diagnosed with gestational diabetes, which was probably caused by my bread and milk diet, so my gynecologist advises me to stop eating carbs and sugary fruits. Normally, cutting carbs out of my food was never a problem, but... I am pregnant, in winter, and the Chrismas market is already open, and I love the hand-made Nussnougat bars, and the Feuerwurst that comes in a Sandwichbrötchen, topped with Tsatsiki and Krautsalat. That's why excluding carbs from the menu is tougher than expected. In the end, I somehow manage to resist the temptation, and I survive the sugar-detox because I want to be a healthy mom, with a healthy baby.

Throughout the second trimester of my first pregnancy, I start experiencing nocturnal orgasms during sleep. They actually come as a bonus to the intense orgasms I feel while having sex. Surprisingly, being pregnant turns out to have a positive effect on my sex life as it is so damn easy to orgasm! We keep on making love almost every day, and I totally enjoy it, even if my belly feels and looks really weird afterwards.

Unfortunately, there are some potential problems lurking around the corner, so relaxing during the last months of my pregnancy turns out to be a mission impossible.

We are living in a small furnished apartment, very cozy and perfect for a young couple, but not for a family. We try to find a bigger flat, but since it's a difficult year for the rental market in Schwabendream (huge demand, small offer) finding something turns out to be really complicated. And, due to my situation at the time, we have to accept an apartment that is not our best, but our only option...

We end up moving to our new home in the last week of November, when I am already extremely pregnant (my due-date is January 10th). As you can imagine, we have a lot of work to do and, even if we are happy to start a new chapter in our life, the moving itself is incredibly stressful, especially because the new apartment isn't furnished, not even the kitchen! That means we have to buy and build our own furniture in less than a month. And since we are sort of alone in Germany, I don't have the luxury to sit down, relax, and enjoy my big belly. Instead, I'm on my knees, scrubbing, mopping, and dusting. I feel the urge to clean and organize everything. It's like an invisible force that's motivating me to transform our flat into a nice, child-friendly home, a perfect nest for our unborn baby. And, of course, after all that work, she came earlier than expected!

The 'normal' birth experience

When I say 'normal' birth, I mean vaginal birth. Vaginal birth doesn't mean natural birth. I learned that the hard way!

The term 'natural birth' is very popular nowadays and it somehow manages to blur pregnant women's expectations, by selling them a dream delivery, and by filling their heads with lies. Natural birth and vaginal birth are not the same! The chances of experiencing a natural, non-medicated birth are extremely low. So let's just stop fooling ourselves. Let's prepare for reality instead.

Why do doctors and midwives make it sound like it's a piece of cake? Yes, every woman has a vagina, and every woman can try to deliver her baby vaginally. Some might experience a relatively easy birth, others might be left handicapped for life.

The shape of the female pelvis varies a lot. We all know that the pelvic area is a flexible structure which allows us, mothers, to birth our babies vaginally.

But, it's important to remember that some women have a wider pelvis and hips that might make it easier for them to expel a baby from their uterus, while other women suffer from birth canal issues, which can make vaginal delivery very difficult.

Unfortunately sometimes we, mommies-to-be, are too naïve and not prepared for giving birth (emotionally and physically). So we end up allowing doctors and midwives to poison us, and our babies, with a cocktail of chemicals. And when we come back to reality, and realize we have been lied to, it's usually too late to change anything.

Are you familiar with the phrase 'Scientia potentia est'? That should be your motto if you are considering giving birth to your baby vaginally, in a German health facility. Why is that so important? Because if you don't know your rights while in hospital, you don't have any!

Be aware of all the 'interventions' used by health professionals throughout a vaginal delivery. They won't ask your permission because they consider it routine. Well, at least that's the case in Germany...

Don't allow them to take control over your body because they don't actually care about you, or your baby. You are unique, your needs are unique, try to remember that, and be aware that you have options. You can refuse their medical advice if you are healthy and feel like doing it.

✳✳✳✳

Motherhood is considered to be part of a woman's human nature but, from the moment her baby is conceived, her life is completely altered. Pregnancy can be really frustrating since every pregnant woman is under the power of her pregnancy brain. She might struggle to remember details, or stay focused, because she is exhausted, and possibly overwhelmed, by the idea that a small human will come out of her vagina, and her life will permanently change. She is fragile because there is so much going on inside her body. That's why you should never criticize a pregnant woman.

Instead, try to be there for her, be respectful, and help her. Make her feel special and loved. Now is the time to pitch in. Surprise her with breakfast in bed, do the dishes and clean the bathroom. Do something nice for her. Anything is better than just sitting on your ass doing nothing. And even if her favorite sleeping-partner is her huge maternity pillow, you should under no circumstances begin to complain that she doesn't care enough about you. After all, she's the one carrying that baby inside her, while her organs are getting mercilessly kicked and squeezed. She's the one experiencing constipation and hemorrhoids. And let's not forget about the pelvic, vaginal, and rectal pain... She's going through a lot, so please excuse her if she's not in the mood for sex, or if she doesn't allow you to touch her very big, and painful, boobs.

Why don't you give her a massage, instead of being so selfish? I'm sure she'd love to feel your hand caressing her belly, hear you talk to your unborn child, and show that you care.

You should also consider taking a break from booze, and avoid hangovers. This will help your relationship a lot, believe me! It's true that your alcohol consumption doesn't harm the baby in any way but being such a jerk will for sure make your pregnant partner feel scared and alone. Give up booze completely, especially if it's your first baby. If you manage to do that, for her sake and for yours, you will reduce the daily stress levels, and you will help her feel less frustrated. Remember that you're not being a reliable partner if you can't stop drinking during pregnancy. It's annoying, and totally unfair! So, please, be supportive.

This is a hint for you, my dear husband... Do you recall those nasty Christmas parties?? I do! You managed to overdo it, twice, and showed me your evil side ONLY while I was pregnant. WHY?? I never understood why you were so selfish and mean to me. I was feeling completely crushed while you were partying hard. And, after drinking all the available alcohol, you didn't even bother to answer your phone. I was so worried that something bad had happened to you. I cried my eyes out till you decided to come back home. You were too freaking drunk to care about your family. And I still hate you for that! Shame on you, pathetic bastard!

As for you, my beloved mother... even now, when you're in your early 70's, you're still the same selfish, big-mouthed woman. Sadly, you didn't get wiser and more mature with age. You never mentioned anything about girls having periods, growing breasts, masturbating, or having sex. We never discussed relationships, gender issues, pregnancy, or real life situations. When my menstrual cycle came for the first time, I was totally unprepared and overwhelmed. I had to find out everything on my own, before the Internet era, when people relied on books, magazines, and newspapers, to gain information. I went through a lot of crap because you were too freaking shy to talk about it. Stupid, isn't it??

And you, my dear father, you were always away. You never played with us, or read us good night stories. Once, when you were drunk, you told me you didn't actually want to have kids... or a wife. It just somehow happened. You got married because mom was expecting a baby: ME. And back then, in the beginning of the '80, it was a must for the father-to-be to marry the pregnant lady in such a situation. But, honestly, I think you made a big mistake. You two were never good for each other, neither romantically, nor intellectually. You both have complicated personalities, and absolutely nothing in common. You, dear mom and dad, never gave us unconditional love because you probably didn't receive it yourself, and you couldn't understand the need for it. And even now, you don't really enjoy playing with your grandkids. It's absolutely normal for grandparents to be too tired to run after toddlers, I guess. And some people simply just don't want to babysit, or get too involved in their grandchildren's life, but I still think it's unfair...

My brother and I are both C-section babies, and our father was not present when we were born. Both surgeries were medically necessary, and they were planned several months in advance. My mom told me she heard a lot of women screaming with pain while giving birth vaginally, so she was (and still is) very happy that she didn't have to destroy her lady parts.

Since I've also gone through a C-section to deliver my son, I can honestly say it feels like having abdominal surgery, not like giving birth. Yes, the baby will come out of you, and yes the recovery is painful. But, in my opinion, the surgery itself has nothing to do with giving birth. I mean, why should anyone let a doctor cut their belly open, and take their uterus outside, without any medical reason? If labor starts on its own, spontaneously, the pain should be bearable for most women. On the other hand, inducing labor can be very risky, and it can also cause a lot of unnecessary pain because both your body and your baby are not quite ready for birth. So why put yourself at risk unnecessarily? We have to learn to say NO to induction.

If you are pregnant, don't rely on your male-obstetrician to keep you informed about prenatal/postnatal care, and childbirth. Reading stuff about birth is also not enough. You have to perceive the feelings of a real mother in order to understand her emotions, and her fears. And you must learn to calibrate your expectations.

❋❋❋❋

Now, going back to my story... Late December, it's a warm winter, no snow on the ground, just a wave of dark and foggy days. Since I am heavily pregnant, and my hormones are acting really crazy, it sort of feels like Christmas is over before it's even begun.

My parents and my student brother are already in Schwabendream, and we are all impatiently waiting for January to come. Especially me! I hate my heavy body, and I feel so big. I can barely walk because my belly is just too large, even if I weigh only 68kg.

I enjoy spending time with my family but they are totally lazy people. I bust my ass keeping the apartment clean, doing laundry, and cooking. I try to keep my brain busy, so I don't think about what will happen to my body during childbirth. None of my family members, my husband included, gives a damn about my well-being. They seem to really enjoy the holiday season this year.

Suddenly, a growing fear begins to invade my mind. I realize that it's time to come back to reality, after nine months of peacefully living on a cloud, even if I'm not necessarily ready yet for having a baby. I do want my own family but I'm afraid that it will be too complicated, and awkward. I'm feeling disappointed with myself for not being smart enough to figure it out. I'm certainly not happy. Instead, I'm hurting and alone, and no one ever tries to cheer me up. I slowly begin to break apart...

I am very scared of doctors, since forever. When I was a kid they treated my asthma with antibiotic shots that hurt a lot. Thanks to them, even now, I'm terrified of needles. I remember being constantly sick during winter. Sometimes, when it was really cold outside, and the air was frozen and dry, I was barely able to breathe. It felt so weird, as I was the only kid in my school with asthma, and no one seemed to know anything about it back then.

So, here I am, twenty years later, heavily pregnant with my first child. After decades of successfully hiding my fear of doctors, I start revealing my sensitive side, and my massive anxiety about giving birth. I am completely frightened by the thought of having to spend a couple of days in a hospital, surrounded by medical staff. It's perfectly normal to be worried about labor and delivery, but I am paralyzed with fear... Every time when anxiety strikes, it feels like being hit by a bullet train. My heart starts beating very fast and, all of a sudden, I feel very hot and sweaty. I am convinced that something will go awfully wrong, and that I will die in childbirth. I reach out to my family but no one seems to be impressed by my problems. They keep on interrupting me and suggest staying positive.

Honestly, I don't understand why everyone is always talking about positivity. It's perfectly normal to allow ourselves to be unhappy, isn't it? We are complicated human beings and staying positive is just not enough because our life isn't always sunshiny. As rational animals, it is in our nature to be inquisitive, and seek to understand ourselves better. What's going on inside our brains isn't always positive, or pleasant, so why lie about it?

One morning I find myself staring in the mirror once again. I look like a huge deformed balloon, a very sad and unconfident one. I ask my dear husband to take some pictures of my belly but he's never in the mood for it. I want to scream 'I hate you!' and I can hardly stop myself from crying. I crave affection but everyone around seems to ignore my needs. Here I am, in the last days of my first pregnancy, feeling desolate, with no help, or emotional support whatsoever. Shame on you guys! This was supposed to be my special time! I'm not always pregnant, you know!

A few days later, still totally pregnant, I try to convince myself that nothing is wrong with me, and that I will be able to go through a drug-free birth. Maybe my healthy body and the friendly midwives will guide me through labor and delivery, and maybe it will be a unique experience. Did it happen? NO, not even close.

✳ ✳ ✳ ✳

Last week of December... I am on a quest to better understand my emotions. I reach out again to my unfriendly German male ob-gyn but he is not interested in giving any detailed explanations about childbirth, even if he assisted his wife in delivering two babies. Maybe it's impossible for men (even if they work as gynecologists) to understand what pregnancy and childbirth really mean.

Taking part in prenatal classes, watching vaginal birth videos, practicing breathing techniques, and reading about labor and birth, turn out to be a waste of time and energy. 'Why?', you ask. In my case, the midwife hosting the prenatal classes only talks about the obvious things happening during and after giving birth. She doesn't mention a thing about diastasis recti and umbilical hernia, nor does she say anything about postpartum sex problems, caused by the pelvic injuries women usually sustain during vaginal birth. Not once, in any of my prenatal classes, did anyone mention incontinence and pelvic organ prolapse. Why is it still taboo to discuss vaginal health after childbirth? Beats me...

I am tired, huge, and very scared about what is going to happen next. And, surprise, surprise, the next morning, after a very long and exhausting night, my water breaks.

It's around 7am on a Friday. I rush to take a shower and brush my teeth, and then tell everyone what just happened and go directly to see my obstetrician, who doesn't believe me. 'Maybe it's just urine, let me check it first!' he says. A big splash of clear amniotic fluid leaks from my vagina directly on the floor. The ignorant doctor finally believes me and sends me straight away to the local university hospital, where I am about to go through the worst disappointment of my life.

My husband and I arrive there around 10:30am. I am told that I can wait until 6pm before they would have to induce my labor. The situation is bad, my water broke and I feel nothing, no sign of labor whatsoever. We are sent for a walk and I'm hoping that moving around, climbing stairs, jumping, will do something, but it doesn't... I am so hungry but they tell me not to eat anything. So I just drink a lot of water since I'm losing 'water' with every step I take.

A very rude nurse lets us know that we won't get a room for ourselves because we only have public health insurance. 'Sie sind Gesetzlich Versichert, deshalb haben Sie keine Wahlmöglichkeiten hinsichtlich des Krankenzimmers und alle unsere Familienzimmer sind leider belegt!' ('You have public insurance, so you can't choose your room, and unfortunately all our family rooms are occupied!') Her words come as a shock to me. It is hard to accept that I won't get a private room during these scary times. And the worst part is that there is only a tiny bathroom for every two rooms. In other words, one WC for four pregnant female patients plus their birthing partners, and visitors!

I'm extremely pissed that we don't have private health insurance. We opted for the public one because our relocation agent, a chubby German lady, convinced us that the private health plan is better suited for young single people, and that it might easily turn into a trap for families because of the huge costs it actually entails. She also said that going for private and later switching to public is basically impossible, that's why we decided to start with the public one and see how it goes. And to be honest, we were ok with it, until now!

I start crying and keep praying, while my heart is slowly breaking. We are shown to our shared room.

My roommate, a woman in her late 30s, delivered her baby vaginally a few hours before our arrival. It's her second birth, so she already knows what she's doing. She was lucky enough to have the room for herself, until now... She is wearing only a shirt and a pair of disposable undies, and she is trying to breastfeed her newborn baby. We are too embarrassed to wait there for my labor to start, so we decide to go for a walk in the hallways.

I'm a complete mess, desperately trying to keep my shit together. I'm terrified and disappointed at the same time. My body doesn't seem to know how to spontaneously deliver a child. I am completely unprepared for what is about to happen next and, sadly, we are surrounded only by racist medical staff.

My useless husband isn't able to say a word in German, and he's scared as hell. We are told that there is only one doctor on duty in the hospital, and that I should start preparing for induction. I don't insist hard enough, or long enough, for an alternative. At the time, I didn't even know that I had the option to wait a little longer for my labor to start. Eventually, a nurse lets us know 'it's time' and I'm not able to say no to induction.

My labor turns out to be significantly more painful than anything I have ever experienced. My induced contractions are way stronger than expected, and the pain is too intense, and very difficult to manage. And then, the epidural fucks up the whole experience even worse. I am overwhelmed, and I end up losing control over my body...

✻✻✻✻

The standards of behavior during labor in Germany are already set, and every woman is expected to act a certain way. Unfortunately, most hospitals will never allow you to labor in the positions you please, even if it's supposed to be your show. And, although it's proven that all the gravity-positive positions are better for a vaginal birth, they will make you lay on your back, even when you are against it. And, despite the fact that it's your body, it's highly probable that you will NOT be in control of your own birth experience.

However, if you must give birth in a German hospital, don't expect to be treated as an individual but rather as one of the many 'customers' who must use their medical services. For them, it's just a job like any other. They want to finish it as soon as possible, and go home.

Now, let's get a bit into the details of my vaginal delivery, so you can better understand what I mean by that.

11:50am: CTG

1:30pm: CTG + Ultrasound, the one and only ultrasound they performed on me before, during and after labor!

2:30pm: Intravenous penicillin

Since I carry Group B Strep bacteria (or GBS) in my vagina, they decide to put me on IV penicillin. Sadly, I'm not aware and no one mentions the fact that using antibiotics during labor and birth will actually alter my baby's microbiome! A young and inexperienced nurse performs the procedure and, unfortunately for me, she doesn't manage to place the cannula correctly, so she has to do it all over again.

WHAT A JOY! Next step: unblocking the cannula, a really painful process...

We are then left by ourselves for about 4 hours. No one comes to check on me, so we decide to walk around the hospital. And we are walking and talking, and I'm crying, and waiting for my body to figure it out, but, sadly, I still can't feel any contractions whatsoever.

7:00pm: My labor is firstly induced using 50 mg of oral Misoprostol. I am given another 2.5 mg penicillin.

8:00pm: Vaginal exam

I start feeling a lot of discomfort and abdominal pressure. Suddenly, I am experiencing severe stabbing pain in both my pelvic area, and my lower back area. And then, a horrible thing happens. Besides the excruciating pain and discomfort, a really nasty diarrhea hits my bowels and I 'give birth' to a tornado of liquid shit! It's the worst poop of all! It's explosive, and it feels so damn weird, like a cascade of brown dung coming out from my anus, while my entire body is shaking uncontrollably. I feel nauseous and I have to throw up. Poor me!

10:00pm: Vaginal exam

They measure my cervix dilatation and because everything is going too slow (for them!) they decide to make it all go faster. I'm beginning to think that I'm trapped in another dimension. I want to disappear, and get away from all the pain. I close my eyes and slowly open them again... but I'm still here. This shit is real, and it's really happening! I'm living my worst nightmare and I'm petrified.

11:00pm: They give me another dose of 50 mg Misoprostol, without even bothering to warn me about the possible side effects; 2.5 mg penicillin.

No one actually mentioned the risks of administering Misoprostol 'off-label' during labor and delivery and, even if they wrote in the birth report – 'Patientin wurde über Risiken aufgeklärt' (The patient was informed about the risks), neither my husband nor I did receive any explanation as to why it was administered twice. 'Sie bekommen eine kleine Tablette um die Wehen anzuregen' (You will be given a small pill to stimulate labor), that's the only thing they told us. Nothing else was said about the potential side effects of Misoprostol, and no one believed me when I told them that my contractions are too violent to bear. Not even my husband.

12:00am: The real pain starts showing its claws. And it's bad, really bad, 'I'm-gonna-die now!' kind of bad.

Suddenly, my dream of having a natural, drug-free birth is completely destroyed by the sad reality. I have no hope left...

12:30am: Vaginal exam – cervix 1cm dilated; 1 Buscopan suppository

1:00am: Failed water birth attempt – I try going into warm water but it makes no difference, the pain is just awful, and I can't talk or walk anymore.

2:00am: CTG

They stick some Pyonex needles into my lower back region which, by the way, they forget to remove. Two days after delivery, I realize those needles are still there, hurting my skin, and creating bruises.

2:45am: 2.5 mg penicillin

Sadly, the pain is excruciating and I'm not able to bear it any longer. I tell the nurse to give me something, anything. I receive a shot of intramuscular Dolantin but, as expected, it doesn't work. I start screaming loudly, I try all the breathing methods I know, but nothing helps. 'Can you stop screaming? It's embarrassing!' says my STUPID husband. I want to kill him but I can't move.

3:45pm: Vaginal exam – cervix 6-7cm dilated; 1000 ml Jonosteril, intravenous

4:25am: The pain is literally killing me! Then, the inevitable happens: I surrender to the pain and tell the midwife to give me the epidural, or a C-section. She tells me that a C-section is off the table since THE doctor is busy with an emergency case, and because there is no real medical reason for it.

I'm not a religious person, and I don't go to church. I usually visit churches to calm down and enjoy their breathtaking interiors, the vitraux, and the organ sounds. But, this particular night, I feel so lonely, and I suddenly find myself praying, hoping for a miracle to happen. But then, the inexperienced anesthesiology trainee enters the room. And he's not able to stick that catheter in the right spot, so a lot of blood comes out. Unfortunately, he has to do it again, and again...

All my begging is in vain. There is no God, no supreme force, no star, planet, animal. or plant, no one who can hear my prayers and help me get through this pain. Everything fails to work and I'm out of ideas. And my husband can't understand a word of what these people are saying...

Even today, I see it as one of the strongest pain I've ever felt in my entire life, worst that tooth pain, or passing a kidney stone pain. Maybe a bit like simultaneously passing two big kidney stones, after extracting your wisdom teeth! I can't even describe how absolutely terrible and brutal it was.

4:45am: They finally manage to 'install' the epidural in my back, the pain is somehow bearable.

5:00am: CTG pathological! Nobody mentions anything about it! We only find out about this later, from the medical records. Normally, when something abnormal is observed, continuous CTG should be started, which, in my case, didn't happen. Apparently, this is a standard phenomenon often noticed by mothers who gave birth in Deutschland: No one panics about 'the bad hearth-tones'!

5:20am: Another vaginal exam is performed; 1000 ml Jonosteril, intravenous

6:10am: We find out that our daughter changed her position. Poor baby! Filled with painkillers and anesthetics, and stuck inside such a weak mother... Even if I am 10 cm dilated, I'm not allowed to start pushing her out. Instead, the midwife tells me to move inside the bed, in a specific coordinated way, to make my baby change her position again. They call it 'Zilgrei

Übungen'. I start moving up and down in my bed, while my husband stares like a stoned hamster, still not able to understand a word of our conversation in German. I then receive 3 I.E. Oxytocin and 250ml glucose.

6:45am: CTG and 2.5 mg penicillin

6:50am - 8:20am: Several Oxytocin infusions

7:10am: Rectal temperature 38.1C! The midwife tells me to poop, yes, that's right: POOP! But I just can't. 'Stuhl hat ø geklappt!' they wrote in the medical report.

7:10am: I manage to pee, approx. 500ml. I honestly don't know where my pee landed! Spoiler alert! Birth can be a brutal experience if you are not respected by the hospital staff! In my case, five different midwives and nurses came to check on me before I finally got to the pushing phase. Around 7:30am, after a couple of hours of 'hospital-bed-motion', we manage to arrive to a better position, not the optimal one, but good enough to start the pushing phase. When I say not optimal, I'm referring to the occiput posterior position. It means that her face was looking up, toward my abdomen and I can honestly tell you that giving birth to a posterior baby can be absolute agony!

The last midwife, the one who eventually 'helps' me deliver my daughter, keeps telling me that I'm 'useless and pathetic'. She then asks me why would someone like me got pregnant in the first place if I can't give birth the 'natural' way, like a real woman. She also tells me, in a grumpy manner, that I don't know how to push. 'Frau P presst nicht mit voller Kraft und ist wenig kooperativ.' (Frau P does not push with full force and is not very cooperative) I start pushing in a more 'effective' way but it's so damn complicated because I can't breathe properly, lying there on my back! My ginormous belly is pressing on my internal organs and it's making me want to puke. I want to move a little bit but the midwife clearly informs me that I'm not allowed to try different birthing postures because I'm 'too skinny'. So, I'm basically forbidden to move an inch and do what my body is telling me to do. Instead, I'm stuck in the worst position (the best for the midwife!), and I'm pushing like crazy. And the cherry on top are THE NURSES who come out of nowhere and start 'jumping' on my belly. They apply pressure on my abdomen, squeezing the baby out of me with their bare hands, without explaining what they are doing, causing me to freak out and panic. I've never felt so much pain in my entire life! I'm ready to die right now! I'm in hell, and it's awful!

I later find out that this horrifying maneuver, or better said 'pure torture', is called 'the Kristeller-Handgriff' and it's actually an outdated and very dangerous technique that many German hospitals still use as a common practice. It is performed routinely, and without the verbal consent of the patient. My ability to refuse this maneuver was practically nonexistent because no one mentioned anything about it!

One month post-delivery, my belly is still blue and purple, and I'm quite sure there is a connection between the Kristeller maneuver, my diastasis recti, and my umbilical hernia. Shame on you Germany for not prohibiting this harmful technique! 8:29am: The heartless midwife grabs a pair of scissors and is getting ready to cut me. I start yelling for her to stop and then boom! THE TEAR happens... There's tearing everywhere: vagina, perineum, labia, and clitoris. I'm half dead, but I manage to push my daughter out into the world. There she is, in the same room with us, breathless and blue, with the umbilical cord wrapped around her neck.

Why the hell did no one know she had a multiple nuchal cord?? Is it so hard to visualize the nuchal cord's state before going through the pushing phase? Apparently, it was impossible for you, incompetent butchers!

My baby is blue and silent, the cord is wrapped several times around her neck, and she is not breathing. They call someone from the NICU in the delivery room to perform resuscitation. Meanwhile, for a couple of seconds, I feel officially dead, or at least I wish I'd be dead. Two doctors rush in, and start the resuscitating maneuvers. After a couple of minutes, that felt like an eternity, I finally hear her cry. She is alive... I realize I have to come back to life even if I'm completely ready to embrace death.

8:40am: Delivery of the placenta, followed by the stitching up of all the tears.

Forty minutes later, I'm finally holding my precious baby girl. But I'm so damn exhausted, and full of drugs. There we lay, mother and baby, drugged and powerless, trying to understand the terrible and 'wrong' childbirth experience that had nothing natural about it. And my husband, probably deeply shocked by what he had witnessed, is even more useless than before.

After such a disappointing and outrageous vaginal delivery, we are put in a small, dark room, where we can spend one hour together with our newborn baby. And she is very hungry, and I have NO MILK. Wait, WHAT?! Yup, no milk at all...

✳✳✳✳

Dear German midwives and doctors, this is not how I imagined giving birth to my first baby! It's time for you and I to have a talk about childbirth.

First of all, every expectant mother should be treated respectfully, regardless of her race, nationality, and no matter what season we're in: Christmas season is no excuse for poor hospital care! It should be mandatory for medical professionals to educate themselves about PTSD and other traumatic mental illnesses, caused by their lack of morality.

Second, pregnant women should be allowed to choose their 'ideal' birthing position. Every woman is unique, and every human body is different. Maybe my dream birth is totally different from yours. Maybe my legs are longer, and my hips smaller, so maybe I would feel more comfortable in another position than 99% of the women giving birth in the same hospital as I am. So why should I do what YOU say, just because the other 99% did it, instead of listening to my own body?? Pushing a baby out is a big deal, and no one should ever tell an expecting mother HOW she should get through childbirth. I'm sure it's possible for all healthy women to give birth vaginally without having to experience a great loss of control, and without having to change their birth plan completely.

Unfortunately, we're constantly being put under pressure to do something we don't want to do, so that the birth would happen fast, even when that means unnecessary pain and suffering.

If you would sacrifice five minutes of your precious time, and give us a simple explanation for each procedure at each stage of labor, and the reason why you must do it, our birth experiences would be smoother, and more natural.

We, ordinary women who didn't study medicine, put our trust in your ability to guide us through the birth process. And what do we get in return? We are treated disrespectfully, and it's really unfair! Nobody actually takes time to make us feel safe, and nobody bothers to make sure we have a decent birth experience.

Why do you expect us to know the types of medical procedures and their names? We are not doctors, and we owe you nothing! Why do you prefer ignorance over compassion? Do you really enjoy deceiving millions of women by treating them like animals? Why must a pregnant woman feel violated and deprived of her human dignity during childbirth? Why do you enjoy behaving in such a barbaric way? And why the hell do we even pay you, while you continue treating us like crap? Why is it so hard to understand that each and every woman is distinct, every birth experience is powerful and emotional, and it can lead to trauma if not properly handled? Why are most labors induced?

Why is the epidural placed too early, or too late? Why is everybody talking about natural, unmedicated birth, if no doctor really understands it? Why is it acceptable to treat psychological damage instead of preventing it? It is always THE WOMAN'S birth experience that matters, not yours! Shame on you, despicable people! No one should feel humiliated and mistreated during childbirth!

✺✺✺✺

Before actually giving birth to our daughter, I am convinced that I will be overwhelmed with unconditional love, the moment I'll hold her in my arms. But guess what? I'm not! In fact, I feel overwhelmed with something else: FEAR and GUILT... Nothing went as planned, and nothing is as I imagined it would be. I'm lying in the hospital bed, with a screaming baby on my chest, trying my best to breastfeed her, and my entire body hurts like hell.

Where is the JOY, where is the fulfillment? Why am I feeling so lost and alone, even if my husband is here with me? You, my dear husband, are standing there, just like all the other pieces of furniture in the room, silent, and useless. Your eyes are totally empty, no sign of pride, or love, no kisses, or hugs. Thank you again for NOT being there when I really needed you!

My last meal was more than 24 hours before and I'm still on drugs. I feel like a zombie coming back from the dead. I'm clueless, scared, and convinced that I'm the only one to blame for all the postpartum-problems I'm facing.

My daughter won't latch and I'm not producing enough milk. It's something new to both of us, and it seems like the most complicated thing in the world. I'm so frustrated...

A young nurse enters the room and she tells me to try again, and again, and again, and I do, but nothing comes out. My baby girl is crying her eyes out, and it's freaking crazy because no one seems to give a damn about us. However, they mention 'More than two hours of breastfeeding support' in the hospital report. You shameless liars!

My breasts hurt like hell, so I start squeezing them and some colostrum comes out. My daughter is able to drink enough to put her hunger on hold. She goes to sleep soon after I put her in her crib. I don't feel like keeping her close to me. Everything went beyond wrong, and I'm completely disappointed. I feel miserable and I fear that I won't be able to keep up with the demands of a newborn. Nothing seems logical anymore, I desperately need help...

A couple of minutes later, we are moved to our shared maternity room. My roommate, who delivered her baby the day before, has visitors. Entering a room full of strangers was never one of my strengths, so, as you can imagine, I immediately get hit by a huge panic attack. I'm half naked, with a lot of weird bloody stuff coming out of my shredded vagina. It's so damn intimidating. What a joy! I love it! Ok, ok, they might all be nice people, welcoming a new family member. But still, they are just too many, and too loud for one shared postpartum hospital room. Having a roommate it's ok, but having her family over, without any notice whatsoever... what the heck, you weird German people? Not cool!

Soon after that awkward and embarrassing encounter, I manage to eat something while our baby girl is still asleep. Around 7pm, my brave husband decides he had enough of 'the baby experience' for one day. He is very tired (just him, not me!) and decides to head home. Five minutes later, he actually leaves me there alone, in my misery. And he doesn't feel guilty at all, at least not before I mention it to him. In fact, he manages to sleep very well, like a baby. Lucky dude! For me, on the other hand, another nightmare is just about to begin...

It's around 8pm on a cold December evening. A few young midwifery students, some nurses, and one doctor, are the only ones working that night. With just a couple of days left until Silvester (New Year's Eve), I start thinking about the year ahead, and realize that I'm still not ready for my new overwhelming reality. My roommate and her baby daughter are sleeping quietly. I can't sleep since there's a lot of pain going on between my legs. I'm still having abdominal cramps and I'm passing some huge blood clots. My postpartum bleeding is no joke, it feels like my insides are slowly falling out of me.

My daughter wakes up and starts screaming at the top of her lungs. She's hungry, thirsty, and probably afraid of the new scary world she suddenly found herself in. I pick her up and try to breastfeed her but she's not able to latch properly, so she continues to cry her eyes out. Desperate and alone, I call for help. A very unfriendly nurse enters the room. She tells me to change her diaper, and then she vanishes without a trace. Since breastfeeding didn't work, I decide to take the nurse's advice and change the diaper. My entire body hurts like hell, I'm struggling to stand up, and I'm barely able to move around. I'm crying in silence so I don't bother my roommate. Eventually, I somehow manage to change my daughter's diaper. Don't ask how! For the record, it's nothing like changing a baby doll's diaper! (...the only thing I was familiar with) Once the clean diaper is in place, she stops crying for a while. But the silence doesn't last long because she's hungry, and I don't know how to breastfeed her. Yes, that's right, I don't know how! I squish her tiny face into my breasts, trying all the techniques I practiced during the prenatal classes, but nothing works. I decide to look for help again. I gently put my screaming baby in her wheeled crib, and start pushing her through the hallway. My clothes are soaked in blood. I'm literally leaving traces of blood behind me, while my dear husband is sleeping like a baby. I finally manage to find someone, a young nurse who doesn't seem to know more than I do about breastfeeding. My daughter's face is red like a tomato. I'm desperate, so I start begging for some formula. I can actually feel the nurse's disgust through the way she looks down upon me, but honestly, I don't give a rat's ass! I take the formula and feed it to my baby right away. She finally calms down.

It's already 2am. My roommate and her newborn baby are still sleeping in silence. One hour later, things go crazy again. So, here I am, walking through the long and creepy hospital hallway, trying to find the young nurse so I can ask her for help, again. But honestly, how is she supposed to help me when she obviously doesn't have children of her own? Anyway, she's my only option...

Feeding and changing the diaper are useless, so the young nurse suggests wrapping my daughter in a blanket, so she can feel 'like a baby in the womb'. She then complains that I'm too needy and reminds me, in a scorching tone, that she's working alone, and has other patients to take care of. Unfortunately, the burrito-like baby wrapping style doesn't satisfy my daughter's needs, so she starts screaming again.

It's 5am... after almost 48 hours without sleep, I'm officially in a deep zombie state, pushing my daughter's crib through the hospital's hallways, crying and admiring her tiny face, and her big blue eyes. She's charmed by the neon lightning so she finally stops crying. I decide to spend the rest of the night here, walking and dragging my bleeding body behind me, just like a wounded animal.

Around 8am, my dear husband comes to visit us, after a refreshing night of sleep. The moment I see his face, I know I hate him so much! I tell him everything about our long and exciting first night. He just can't accept the fact that I haven't slept at all, and that no one helped me. He strangely believes that being in the hospital is the best option for us, and sees it as a positive experience, since, you know, Germany has such good hospitals. He also has some important 'news' for us.

After talking to his parents, he decides to let me know that his family doesn't like the name we chose for our daughter, and hope that we will change it. Now, imagine my face, when I hear 'the news' coming from him, my beloved husband, who abandoned us in that inhumane German hospital.

'You're playing with me, right?' I ask him. 'No, I'm serious.' he replies, visibly embarrassed.

WTF?? You ignorant mama's boy! What a good moment you picked to place your family's opinion above mine! I can't believe my ears! I'm full of rage and sadness! I just want to kill him and his family too! Shame on you, stupid people! You should have never made mean comments about our daughter's name. It's not weird, silly, or illegal! You deceived me greatly and I'll never forgive you!

I feel so small and insignificant, like a piece of shit, so all I can think about is DIVORCE. In the end, I somehow manage to keep my calm, and decide to give my husband another chance, since he's the father of my baby. And, of course, I didn't change our daughter's name because I love it, and it just fits her like a dream. Every time I say it, or hear it, I know I picked the right one.

Because the hospital is almost empty, and since my roommate decided to head home, we eventually get the room for ourselves. My husband has no excuse left, he must spend the night with us. So, after 52 hours, I finally get the chance to SLEEP.

The next morning, after digging into the hospital breakfast, I'm ready to give breastfeeding another try. An older nurse comes to check on us. She suggests that I try different positions and different breast holding techniques, but no matter what we do, it doesn't work. After a while, another nurse enters the room and she just stares at my naked breasts. 'Well, with nipples like that you can't breastfeed your baby!' she says with a hint of sarcasm. She then throws me a case containing a pair of nipple shields. At first, her attitude upsets me, but then, I realize she might be onto something. Sadly, breastfeeding with nipple shields turns out to be really painful, so I decide to start pumping my milk. One of the nurses brings an electric breast pump. I'm advised to use it every three hours.

After pumping for about 25 minutes, my breasts suddenly feel heavy, and very painful. Within a couple of hours I realize I'm full of milk. I keep on pumping, and feed my daughter my pumped milk from a bottle. Soon after, I notice that my nipples are bleeding but, because I have such a huge amount of milk inside me, I decide to keep on doing it, no matter how painful it is.

On December 31st around 4pm, we are released from the maternity unit. NO perineal examination is carried out, and I receive no postpartum care advice whatsoever. I decide to borrow the electrical pump from the hospital, even if I'm secretly hoping that my breastfeeding problems will go away the moment I'd step foot inside our apartment. Sadly, my postnatal midwife turns out to be a complete idiot!

YOU, dumb midwife, came to my house on January 2nd and cut my stitches assuring me that a 'natural healing' was the best thing for my body. And I let you do it, STUPID ME! Later on, I discovered a piece of flesh that resembled a tongue hanging out of my vagina. More about this in the next pages…

You also didn't listen to any of my questions, and didn't take time to fully understand my breastfeeding struggles. You were always in a rush so you suggested continuing using the pump and the bottle. YOU ARE THE WORST! I hate you so much, I will always do! Your lack of knowledge destroyed me physically, and mentally, you incompetent fool!

****

Motherhood, week one: the worst decision I make, after coming back home from the hospital, is to keep sleeping in the same bed with my husband. His snoring wakes the baby, not just me! However, I am way too sleep-deprived to notice what's really going on, so we never talk about this. My husband sleeps his nights peacefully while snoring like a truck's engine, and he goes to work every single day, as if nothing important happened in our lives.

As for me, I'm pumping milk every three hours, 24/7... Breastfeeding is the best way to bond with your baby, but keep in mind that it can also be a real challenge. It's a complicated 'business' for some of us, and it would definitely help if we would start talking more openly about our breastfeeding issues, and maybe even start teaching it in schools. Don't feel bad and guilty if you can't do it properly. Formula doesn't have all the benefits of breastmilk, but it's not poison!

My parents and brother are also acting like nothing changed. They are just being themselves, selfish, as usual. My mother's only wish is to hold the baby. I'm sure she sees it as a way of helping me, but she is actually 'stealing' my daughter from me. Just to be clear, my girl and I have no space, or time, to bond properly, and my mother doesn't see the damage she is causing us.

My student brother is too young and immature to fully understand the situation, so he packs his things, and flies away the next morning.

Two days later, my father decides to travel back home because it's all too boring for him.

Eventually, after my mother returns home as well, I realize what a huge mistake I made by inviting my family to spend time with us.

The first month after delivery must be only about you and your new baby! Believe me, we did that when our son was born, and it was amazing. Nobody else should be nearby, if you want to be able to focus on your newborn, and to successfully complete your healing journey. The mere presence of other people will take away your energy and time, making it difficult to keep your head above water. Our bodies need time to properly recover, and our minds need even more time to process the pain, and accept the new reality.

Just to be clear, I still remember every single detail of both traumatic births I've been through, and it's still a massive effort for me to properly hide the deep scars left behind. They say you forget everything about your painful delivery after your baby is placed on your chest for the first time, but that's just a big fat lie. Why is everyone trying to hide the truth? Why is it so important to keep pregnant women in the dark?

Motherhood, week five: after a long struggle, the old-me is finally gone. The image of the blue baby and the burdens of the last month must have scared the shit out of her, so she decided to vanish.

Sometimes, when I drink enough alcohol, I can still catch a glimpse of that naïve and idealistic young woman, but she never stays after the hangover is gone. The new-me, whom she left behind, feels overwhelmed with what's going on. I'm drowning in emotions, slowly falling apart, and I don't know what to do about it. My demons are constantly telling me that I'm not a good mother, and that I don't deserve to live. I start having vivid nightmares about my daughter's delivery. The same bad dream keeps repeating itself over and over again. I'm afraid to fall asleep because, every time I shut my eyes, all I see is blood, and a blue baby with the cord around her neck... Every night I am transported to the same white hospital room, lying in the same birthing bed, filled with hate and covered in blood, my blood. The scary midwife is violently cutting my flesh while two other women are jumping on my stomach, and I'm crying, and screaming, asking them to forgive me for being so weak. And then, the blue baby comes out and sits on my chest. I can't move or speak. I can feel her heavy weight on top of me, crushing the air out of my lungs. It hurts so badly! When I finally manage to wake up, my heart is racing and I'm sweating like I ran a marathon.

I'm also experiencing intrusive thoughts about my baby dying in different ways: falling from the crib, me dropping her from the balcony, some bad person stealing her for her organs, or raping her. I'm terrified that she could suffocate, or choke on milk. Besides all this, I'm imagining all kinds of scenarios involving fires, car crashes, and even ghosts, and monsters. And every time the story ends the same way: I'm incapable of saving my baby.

My life slowly turns into a horror movie set. I'm barely getting some rest. By the 14th sleepless night I'm officially a zombie. This time around, it's a different species of zombies, a suicidal one, since my 24/7 hobby is imagining new ways of killing myself. I feel like a complete failure as a person, and I'm ready to put an end to my miserable existence. My pain is too deep and way out of control. Every time I see a knife, I feel a diabolic need to stick it in my belly. It's an incredibly strong urge to hurt and kill myself in order to escape my painful reality.

Luckily, one day, after looking into my baby's eyes and picturing her future without a mother (surrounded by my husband's family), I decide to hide all the knives we have in our kitchen. I also start meditating.

Our daughter might be a very happy and joyful baby but that's not enough. I need help... I try talking to my husband but he doesn't seem to understand anything. My obstetrician is actually very surprised to hear about my struggles because, apparently, all his German patients are aware that childbirth is not a beautiful experience, and they know how to get over it quickly. He also tells me to stop using the pump because 'pumping is not breastfeeding'. 'You should switch to formula as soon as possible' he says. On that specific day, I promise myself I won't go see him ever again. And I manage to keep my word, until I get pregnant again. I know I should have tried to find another doctor, but I'm so scared and embarrassed about having to show my shredded lady parts to a stranger...

I also try talking to a couple of midwives, hoping that their knowledge would help me better understand my new reality. One of them praises the greatness of German mothers, who are not so easily affected by childbirth. They enjoy their new lives, and feel happy and proud because they have birthed healthy babies. Another midwife tells me that I should be grateful for being given 'the opportunity to experience childbirth in Germany, and not in some poor country!' Needless to say, their advice is more discouraging and demotivating than helpful.

My life is a complete mess, and I'm left with so many questions without answers. It feels like I'm stuck in a dark hole and my baby girl is my only reason to stay alive. I have to find a way out of my own hell but I'm not ready yet to see a shrink... I start doing some research, asking other non-German mothers about their birth stories, and trying to find some logical explanations to comfort my mind.

It takes me years to finally figure out a way to navigate through my traumatic childbirth experience, years of not being able to speak about it, years of complete loneliness and suffering behind closed doors. And then, all of a sudden, I'm able to control my emotions. Although there are some triggers I have to be aware of, if I want to stay away from that scary void (people, especially C-section moms and doctors, reading or watching something about pregnancy and babies, certain events and holidays), I'm definitely in a better place than I was a few years ago. However, there are days when it's hard to keep my head up, when I turn into an emotionally unstable weirdo. I start crying out of the blue, and I can't stop. I desperately beg for another chance. I just want my body and my life back. I keep asking myself: Why me? Why my baby? And then I stop, and I realize it's all in the past, and it can't be changed. Slowly, my mind gets invaded by fear, and I dream of dying again, while embracing a moment of emptiness. No sadness, no anger, just an eternal passage through silence. Suddenly, nothing matters anymore. No one, and nothing, can bring me down. My brain starts wandering into dangerous territory and I realize I can't remember anything from my daughter's first year of life, apart from her traumatic birth. As crazy as it might sound, I find it hard not to feel a sense of distress every time I look into her eyes. Her cute face is a constant reminder of that terrifying night. I loved her from the moment I met her and I still do, and I know she is not responsible for what happened to me, but the pain is still there. It has always been difficult for me to celebrate her birthday. But I hope, someday, I will eventually see it as a happy event. For now, December and January are still the worst months of the year, and it's crucial that we don't stay home. When I see Christmas decorations, my pulse starts racing and my breathing gets shallow, as a flush of anxiety rushes through my body. And when the 28th of December arrives, the terrifying nightmares return to haunt me once again. I start reliving every moment, every second of agony, and I can't stop glancing at the clock. And when the clock finally reads 8:29am, the nausea overwhelms me, my stomach aches like hell, and my lungs are being suffocated by the vivid flashbacks.

Every year, I am determined not to fall apart again, and every single time I fail to do so. Not being able to celebrate my daughter's special day is so damn frustrating! I feel so guilty...

With our son, on the other hand, things are totally different. My heart pounds with excitement and joy, in the days approaching his birthday. His delivery was also a traumatizing experience for me, but I somehow managed to understand the necessity of the pain I went through while birthing him.

The C-section birth Experience

After three long years of struggling with postpartum trauma, the idea of having another baby doesn't seem so bad anymore. Suddenly, I feel full of hope. Maybe life is giving me another chance to heal my wounds and substitute the painful memories surrounding the birth of our first baby with more pleasant ones.

When our daughter is 30 months old, I start thinking about having a second baby. This time around, I am far more educated, and I already understand what traumatic labor and delivery mean. Besides this, I have no expectations whatsoever from my family because I know they will fail to support me once again.

Research shows that having one child makes a woman happier than not having children at all. It feels weird to say this, but in my case, giving birth to our first baby didn't make me happy. Instead, it took away the trust and love I once felt for myself, and left me paralyzed with guilt and sadness. That's why, in the beginning, having a second child seems like a pretty bad idea in general. But, even if I'm conscious that birthing another baby would most likely take all the emotional energy I have left, it still appears like a possible salvation for the suicidal part of my brain. Besides that, I've always wanted two kids because I grew up with my brother, and it's wonderful to have a playmate and a true friend, to learn from each other and to share beautiful memories.

In the end, after considering all the pros and cons, I'm very pleased with my decision to get pregnant again. I immediately approach my husband about it, as rationally as possible. He is aware of my 'scars' and he loves having unprotected sex, so he agrees right away. We are both more mature now (well, at least we think so), and we know that having another baby could be beneficial for our relationship in the long run.

I have to mention that our sex life changed radically after having our daughter. The lack of sleep, the new challenges, my depression, and my shredded genitalia, made us feel like the flame was gone.

My vulva was always my best friend, but after vaginally delivering our daughter, things didn't feel right down there. I was, and still am, incredibly insecure about my lady parts. Some pieces of my labia are missing, and there is flesh coming out of my vagina, making my life very miserable sometimes. I try to ignore my 'vaginal tongue' as much as I can. My genius gynecologist wants to remove it but that won't happen any time soon, since I'm not willing to let him (or any other doctor) go near my muff again.

Having sex with a purpose, making love to make a baby, has a different meaning and it feels magical. It's a rare attempt at reviving our sad sex life, and it turns out to have a positive impact on my mental health as well.

One sunny morning, during our Italian summer vacation, I suddenly feel pregnant again. I decide to take a test to confirm my suspicion and it comes up positive, and so does the second one. I am so delighted, and so grateful that I'm pregnant, but honestly, I somehow know this feeling won't last long. A couple of weeks later, I start having cramps. I sit on the toilet and a lot of blood comes out, most of it looking like big clots (pink, red and brown). It feels like a very painful period, but after a few hours it turns into a lighter bleeding. Several days later, I ask my obstetrician if I should worry about it. He advises me to start having unprotected sex whenever I'm ready, if I wish to get pregnant again. He also mentions that miscarriages are certainly disappointing and sad, but also very common during the early weeks of pregnancy, and that a woman can suffer a miscarriage without even realizing she's pregnant.

One year later, still not pregnant, I start panicking a bit... I was never a calm person, I might even win a prize for overthinking everything. That's why not being able to get pregnant again turns my whole world upside down. So, naturally, I start doing my own research about fertility treatments.

There are a lot of suggestions everywhere but since I'm too afraid to see a specialist (I just don't trust doctors), I decide to try a plant based tincture made from Heracleum sphondylium, which helps regulate my heavy, irregular periods. I also start eating meat again, after more than two years of vegetarianism under my belt. Besides that, I stop going to the gym completely, even if I do love my workouts. Three months after regularly taking the tincture, eating meat, and having a lot of unprotected sex, I finally feel pregnant again, and manage to stay pregnant.

Compared to my first pregnancy, when I was nauseous all the time and got the gestational diabetes that made me cut my carbs intake by almost 90%, this second pregnancy turns out to be way more difficult. I'm still feeling nauseous but, on top of that, I start throwing up every day, usually in the evening. I can't drink anything... really, nothing. I'm getting sick just by looking at liquids. I can only eat raw and smoked sausage. I know that there is a risk of getting toxoplasmosis if you eat raw and undercooked meat, but my stomach just craves sausage. And, luckily for me, we are living in the land of the Wurst!

This time around, my pregnancy diet is a very weird one, and it takes a couple of months until I'm able to eat properly again. Unfortunately, after not drinking enough liquids for a while, I end up having low levels of amniotic fluid. Nevertheless, my belly is still very big, and very round and, because it puts a lot of pressure on my internal organs, I'm constantly feeling pain in my lower abdominal area.

One day, I kindly ask my dear husband to act like a mature adult, and help me more than he did during my previous pregnancy. And guess what? By mid-December, he completely forgets all his promises and decides to disappoint me, once again. After attending a Christmas party, he stops answering his phone and comes home in the morning, drunk, like an idiot. I cry till 2am thinking about his stupid behavior, and imagining all sorts of bad things happening to him. I'm so pissed and upset, my anger keeps me awake till 5am when I finally hear his footsteps in the hallway. The moment I see his drunken face, I just want to kill him right away. It feels like déjà-vu, but this time we are parents, so I don't make a scene about it because I don't want to wake up our daughter. Apparently, getting totally wasted while his wife is heavily pregnant is my husband's hobby. Once again, shame on you, ungrateful and ignorant moron! I still hate you for ruining my pregnancies.

✳✳✳✳

Our son is due at the end of March. At the beginning of January we find out that he is stuck inside my belly in a very bad breech, almost transverse, position.

Because of my low amniotic fluid levels, I'm put under medical surveillance and get my baby checked every other day. Having to visit the hospital so often really starts fucking with my mind, making me very frustrated, scared and unhappy.

My demons begin to show their claws again. I urgently need to set a goal and rationalize my actions, to be able to go through these challenging times without going crazy. That's when I decide to do everything in my power to turn the baby in the right position, even if my dream of experiencing a natural birth appears to be less and less achievable, again.

To be completely honest, I also dream of a repaired vulva! And a 'normal' delivery could give me the opportunity to get rid of my vaginal tongue once and forever.

I manage to find an older midwife, who practices acupuncture. We also do moxa sticks, the smelly burning sticks that are supposed to stimulate some important points located at the outer edge of each little toe. Besides that, she suggests trying some special yoga postures, aimed to make enough space in my belly for the baby to move. It feels very weird and uncomfortable, and I have to do it for at least one hour, every day. On top of that, I decide to see a chiropractor who tries to track my baby's kicks and align my body parts in such a way that my son would 'decide' to flip in the right position. He believes that if the right environment is created, the baby can help itself. But, of course, nothing works...

So, here I am, at the beginning of March, totally sad and discouraged. My last resort is the external cephalic version and, after properly analyzing its pros and cons, I decide to give it a shot.

Instead of accepting the fact that I was carrying a breech baby, I chose to hate my body once again.

When I think about all the effort and energy I put into turning our son, all the emotional stress, all the anger. It was such a shitty experience. Fortunately, I also learned that I'm stronger than I thought I was.

Let me give you some details about this brutal and painful procedure that can leave your belly full of bruising. Honestly, even if I do know some successful stories, I can't recommend it to anyone.

March 6th. My husband and I arrive at the hospital around 8am. We are both nervous as hell. I am told to change into a hospital gown and be emotionally prepared for an emergency C-section, just in case. We are then moved to a delivery room where we have to wait for the doctor who will perform the 'magical' procedure. A young nurse enters the room. She tells me to lie down and keep calm. Our son's heart rate is monitored for half an hour, to be sure that he's doing ok. Then, the nurse inserts an IV into my right arm and I'm given some medication used to inhibit uterine contraction (tocolysis). After a while, a friendly female doctor joins us and she double-checks our son's position via ultrasound. She coats my belly with a lot of gel, and then attempts to turn our breech boy. I'm scared. I close my eyes and grip my husband's arm. I can feel the doctor's hands pressing on my bump, her fingers digging 'inside' my abdomen, trying to grab our son's head and bottom, and slowly flip him around. The first attempt, clockwise, is too painful for me, so she tries to move him in the other direction. Unfortunately, the second attempt is only half way successful, since she only manages to move his head. His bottom is stuck, apparently. She asks me to relax, and we decide to give it another try. Warm tears are flowing on my face and my heart is racing like a sports car. It's so damn painful and I just can't relax while my belly is squeezed like a lemon. After the 4th attempt, we decide to stop since we already know that my amniotic fluid levels are low, and don't want to risk distressing the baby too much. The doctor concludes that it's too risky to try performing the procedure again, and she suggests scheduling my unavoidable C-section for the next morning. Wait, what? I panic... not only because of the C-section itself, but because my mother in law was born on March 7th, and I despise this woman. I know, it's crazy, but I totally refuse to give birth to my son on her birthday!

After seeing my teary reaction and hearing my explanations, the doctor seems to understand what's going on inside my head and gives me one last option: March 10th. And, since going back to the university clinic is out of the question, I accept without hesitation.

The moment we are out of the hospital, I start crying and I can't stop. I realize I have three days left to get used to the idea of surgery. I'm pretty upset and still hoping for a miracle to happen. And, because time is flying so fast, I decide to try inducing my labor at home, by drinking one liter of raspberry-leaf-tea daily.

Our son's heart rate still needs to be monitored, so the next day, when I tell one of the nurses about the tea, she looks me straight in the eyes and says 'You have to stop, it's too dangerous! If you're a good mother, you will calm down and accept your situation.' The guilt hits me like a tsunami and I finally see how stupid I am. I break down in tears...

During the night, I can't sleep, I keep thinking about the surgery, and I'm convinced I will die the next day. I decide to sneak out of bed and write a letter to my daughter, explaining what happened, and telling her how much I loved her, and how grateful I am to have her in my life. I then manage to cry myself to sleep...

✼✼✼✼

March 10th, the big day is here.

6am: We arrive at the hospital, park our car, and grab our bags.

7am: I am already naked on the table of torture, crying, and imagining the worst outcome. A nurse inserts a catheter into my bladder and it burns like hell. I can't believe it's happening again... another excruciating childbirth experience!

7:20am: I am surrounded by doctors, anesthesiologists, and nurses, a team of almost 10 persons who are staring at my naked body. No familiar face among them, not even the doctor who supervised us and performed the external cephalic version. Just wonderful! I cry like an emo, and I can't keep my shit together. My husband has to wait outside for now.

A very friendly nurse starts talking to me, trying to help me overcome my fears and demons. She's wearing a surgical mask, like all the others, so I can't properly see her face. But her voice and her joyful eyes give me so much comfort. She then shows me how to bend over for the spinal to be administered.

7:40am: The anesthesiologist explains what will happen next. He then begins the procedure. I am laid on my back and the nurses are hanging a drape to provide a sterile operating field. My husband is allowed to come in and sit by my head. He's with me, finally! This time around, he's a bit more helpful, considering that he is now able to understand German, and even engage in a simple conversation.

One of the doctors asks me if I can feel anything from my waist down, and then announces that she'll make the first incision. There are two or more different conversations going on between the doctors and nurses. I'm still crying and feel like my whole world is collapsing. The uterine incision is then made and I start feeling some pressure.

8:21am: Our son is cut out of my uterus and, luckily, I can hear him cry right away. What a relief!! They briefly show him to me. The moment I see his face I realize

I'm totally in love with him. He's such a gorgeous big baby, 3,800 kilograms and 56 cm long. Compared to our daughter, who went from blue to red skin after being delivered vaginally, his skin is so white and his face has no wrinkles.

My husband is called to the room next to the OR, where he can stay with the baby until I'm stitched up.

The surgery – 'Primäre Sectio caesarea modifiziert nach Misgav-Ladach' – lasts a bit longer than expected because, when they cut my belly open, the skin tears up so badly that they have to work a lot to make the scar look human. Even today, a couple of years after it happened, I still have a big ugly scar on my abdomen, nothing like those cute, tiny celebrity C-section scars. 9:40am: Once I'm finally sewn up, I'm given some Cytotec, via my butthole, to reduce the blood loss. Everyone in the OR congratulates me, and says goodbye. I'm then moved onto a bed, and rolled into our shared room.

Since that's my second delivery, I already know I don't want to be left alone in a German hospital. I'm totally frustrated and freaked out because I just went through major surgery to birth our son. So I make it clear to my husband that he must stay with us, no matter what happens, even if, once again, we didn't manage to get a family room. One hour after the surgery, the pain kicks in, and I'm only given Ibuprofen and Paracetamol...

In the meantime, a young woman in labor checks into our shared room. Her partner quickly leaves their luggage on the bed, and they go directly to the delivery room. Since I'm in so much pain, I barely notice their presence.

After going through a disastrous breastfeeding journey with my daughter, I quickly decide I won't even try breastfeeding our son. Two nurses unsuccessfully attempt to convince me that breastfeeding is the most natural thing. After hearing their opinions, I let them know that my decision is final. Eventually, they bring us some formula.

Around noon a very rude and arrogant old nurse comes in to check my wound, and take my vitals. I ask for some extra pain medication but I'm told that taking pills for every little discomfort will have a negative effect on my body. I must endure the pain because every woman who gives birth in Germany does it. Oh, stupid me, I must have forgotten where I was...

Later in the afternoon, the old nurse pays us another visit. She orders me to get out of bed and move around. I know that (theoretically) the quickest way to recover from surgery is to jump out of bed, but I also feel that my body will not be able to move. I decide to share my concerns, but guess what, she quickly lets me know that she doesn't actually care. 'Strong women get out of bed a couple of hours after undergoing a C-section. You have to stand up and walk, NOW!' she says, full of pride and confidence. Since I'm left with no other option, I give my best and try to stand up. And of course, the next second, I'm down on the floor, and I lose consciousness for a couple of seconds. Finally, after witnessing my extraordinary performance, the nurse realizes that I'm not ready to walk yet, and asks my husband to put me back in bed.

During this crappy experience, our son eats his formula, sleeps quietly and doesn't cry. He is the most understanding and wonderful baby. My husband is with us the whole time and he's in charge of all the 'baby work' – changing his diapers, feeding him formula, newborn screening, everything. I'm basically just watching from my bed, feeling guilty, and crying my eyes out.

Around 7pm, my new roommate, let's call her Anna, her partner, and their newborn daughter, enter the room. Or, to be more accurate, her bed is being pushed into the room by a nurse.

The young new mom is exhausted, her partner looks kind or worried, but he seems to be a cool and helpful guy. Their baby daughter is sleeping on her mother's chest like a little angel. We later find out that Anna went through a harsh vaginal delivery, and that she needed an epidural to relieve the agonizing pain after being induced.

It's almost 9pm when a nurse enters our room, looks at us sympathetically, and lets us know that our partners must leave the hospital. Anna and I are both tired and drained, emotionally and physically. We start begging the nurse to let our partners stay with us. 'Normally it's not possible. However, I will make an exception if both of you want this', says the friendly nurse. And why shouldn't she? I mean, it's also helpful for the hospital staff, since our men can move around faster, and take care of the babies.

Few minutes later, our 'not too bad' dinner is brought to us on a tray. I can't really eat, because my abdominal area hurts like hell, and I'm literally full of gas. I can't stop farting and it's so damn painful!

After dinner, we chat a little more with our roommates, and then decide to go to sleep.

Our son sleeps through his first night in my bed. He only wakes up twice to drink some formula. On the other hand, Anna's daughter screams relentlessly all night long. She tries to breastfeed her but it doesn't work. My heart breaks when I see what she's going through. Her struggle brings back some terrible memories. I tell her all about my first delivery and my unsuccessful breastfeeding attempts, but even after hearing my story, Anna still decides to say a categorical NO to formula. However, her partner is very supportive and respectful, and that helps a lot. We somehow manage to get some sleep, while their daughter continues to scream her lungs out for a while, every 30 minutes or so.

By the next morning, Anna realizes that she's not able to walk properly because her buttocks and one of her legs are still very numb. Her partner alerts a doctor who concludes that she suffered some minor nerve damage from the epidural. On top of that, the same doctor warns them that their baby's skin turned 'too' yellow, so even if they are planning to go home, they have to remain in the hospital for at least one more day.

Nevertheless, there's also some good news for all of us: someone checked out and they have a free room! Anna and her partner quickly gather all their belongings and are ready to move to the new room. After a little chat, we say farewell and wish each other a joyful life.

As unbelievable as it might seem, we finally have a room just for us. It's nice to meet friendly people, but nothing compares to having a private bathroom while in hospital! I'm so relieved that I can go and empty my bowels without any spectators. I quickly drink a glass of non-alcoholic beer (it does wonders on my intestines) and go straight to the toilet. Besides a lot of poop and farts, some grapefruit-size blood clots come out and the whole process is very painful. But, after I manage to get the 'devil' out of me, about half of the pain is suddenly gone and I feel so light, like a butterfly.

Three days after the surgery, I'm finally able to move around but I'm still eliminating a huge amount of blood. My biggest blood clot is the size of my baby's head, not joking! I decide to keep it and show it to the nurse but she's not impressed. For her it's just an ordinary boring clot, nothing more, since there's no sign of hemorrhage.

The next morning, I ask my husband to bring our daughter to the hospital, so she can meet her baby brother. The moment she enters the room, I immediately start crying like a helpless little girl. I missed her so much and, fortunately, I'm still alive. I can't describe how overwhelmed with love and gratitude I felt. All my favorite humans were there, with me...

In the afternoon, I finally find the courage to take a short shower and, after putting some fresh clothes on, I decide to give breastfeeding another chance.

Luckily, the atmosphere in this other German hospital is better than expected. The majority of nurses are friendly enough, and some of them seem to genuinely care about their patients. Everyone is thrilled to hear that I'm willing to breastfeed my son, even if they don't really expect me to succeed. I mean, how could my baby switch from the bottle to the breast?! Fortunately, I'm feeling very confident, and to me, that's everything that matters.

I decide to use a pair of nipple shields from the very beginning, even if I'm not a fan, because they feel and taste like a bottle teat, and our son is already used to bottles. And it works! Almost immediately he latches on to my breast. What a joy! I really feel I can actually do it this time, I can breastfeed my baby and not just pump the milk out and put it in a bottle, like I did with our daughter.

Honestly, anything is better for my saggy breasts than the electric pump. I'm still not one hundred percent sure what ruined my boobs: the breast pump, or the pregnancy itself, or maybe a combination of both. I mean, they grew and grew for nine months and then, after they got huge and heavy when the milk came in, they kind of shrunk dramatically, and dropped down. Anyway, I'm quite sure that breastfeeding, the conventional way, with no pump or nipple shields implied, is the best option for keeping your boobs where they should be.

Five days post-surgery, I'm finally allowed to go home. I still need constant help to be able to move and walk, and going up the stairs to the 2nd floor turns out to be the most complicated thing I've ever done (there is no elevator in our building).

The moment we enter our apartment, I send my parents to the airport and by 6pm they're already home. I certainly don't want to relive the bad experience we had when I gave birth to our daughter. That's why we agree to stay alone, just the four of us, and enjoy the new member of our family. Getting to know each other without any outside influence, or pressure, turns out to be the best thing ever!

I also decide to stop using social media for a month (at least). It's nice to be able to fill your free time with real activities. And it gets even more satisfying the minute you stop comparing yourself to your virtual friends.

It's sad... we're so badly intoxicated with this online society we're living in that we forget how to live our real life, on Earth. We seem unable to enjoy the actual, unfiltered colors of nature, and we replaced the beauty of love with unwanted opinions and insecurities. Can you remember the simple, private intimacy, without tweets and online declarations, or giant stone engagement rings photos?

I personally struggle a lot with the social media invasion, and I try to take a break from it as often as possible, even if my cellphone-addicted husband doesn't appreciate my initiative at all.

What's wrong with today's society? Why are so many of us dependent on technology, fast-food, or expensive items that have no real use? Why do we always need more stuff to remain happy, and to be able to enjoy our life? When we travel, we carry a lot of rubbish around and we leave traces everywhere, continuously destroying our planet. We are such big consumers, we devour everything that comes our way. We've become a sort of unsatisfied monsters who are angry at anyone who dares to criticize us. We constantly take and share photos of everything – food, new dress, new shoes, new face, new husband, newborn baby. Yes, sadly, our babies are put on display even before they've opened their eyes...

❋❋❋❋

This time around, I'm feeling happy and grateful. The exhaustion and fear I felt after giving birth to our daughter are gone. Everything is fine so far. It isn't magical because of the surgery, but I'm certainly in a better place.

With the help of my very experienced midwife, after a few days of using the nipple shields, I'm finally able to breastfeed my son 'au naturel'. This lady is a miracle for me compared to the midwife I had after delivering our daughter. She literally pushes the breast inside my son's mouth, and insists until he latches onto my nipple and is able to drink on his own. She is a true professional who takes her job seriously, a friendly and helpful woman, a beautiful mother who birthed three babies of her own. She goes out of her way to show me different breastfeeding positions, and she convinces me not to give up. And boy, it's such a calming and satisfying sensation! It's true that it can also be really painful sometimes (cold cabbage leaves between feedings help a lot), but nothing compares to being so close to your baby!!

New mothers have to live under so much pressure. They are judged for every possible 'mistake' they make, for being fat and unsexy, for not being able to breastfeed properly, or not having a perfect baby who sleeps all night and never cries. And the scary part is that our own mothers and families shame and criticize us the most. They give us 'advice' only to make us feel guilty and insecure.

In our case, the only reason my husband's parents are calling us every other day is to find out if I have enough milk, if the baby is gaining weight, and if he's sleeping his nights. That's it. They don't miss a chance to disguise their judgements as suggestions, and they don't give a shit about me. No one ever asks me how I feel, if I'm in pain, or if I manage to sleep enough. And my husband expects me to stay fit, sexy and happy. WTF?! How can I feel sexy moving around like a drunken snail with these ginormous pads between my legs, soaked in blood? And how about the freaking hemorrhoids happening around my arse? Is that sexy enough?

On top of all this, my diastasis got a lot worse during this pregnancy, and it's currently six fingers wide.

Being a mom is not easy, and given my history with trauma, I do my best to remain calm and hopeful of what the next day may bring. Feeling miserable all the time is not normal, and we shouldn't be embarrassed to talk about our terrifying journey of becoming mothers.

People can be really mean with their rude remarks and insensitive questions. But even if it gets dark sometimes, don't surrender. Try laughter yoga instead and don't be afraid to talk about your struggles. Cry, scream, do whatever it takes. Just don't hide your suffering!

Personal guidance for you

Dear young lady and future mother, as weird as it might sound, you should pay attention to a particular key aspect when it comes to choosing your baby's daddy. In fact, it's something very obvious that we always just kind of forget to take into account: his size. And I'm not talking about his penis. Ok, ok, that 'detail' can also be important, if you want to be able to enjoy certain sex positions. Nevertheless, I'm referring here to his body proportions. That could actually give you a clue about the size of your future babies together. At least, in my case, both our kids were big babies, and are still taller than other kids their age. We always joke that my husband looks like a bear. He's medium tall but his legs are really strong, his calves are very large, and his musculature is impressive. No skinny jeans fit him. He also has a little bit too much body fat, and a big (way bigger than mine) sexy butt. Most likely his body structure was largely determined by genetics, since his father and his paternal grandmother are big people too, both fat and really tall, especially the grandmother who's in her late 80s and already shrunk to 1.80m.

Research suggests that you may be less likely to suffer birth injuries and develop lacerations to your cervix, vagina, or perineum, if you deliver a smaller baby. So, if you want to be able to reach the most appropriate 'baby size' for vaginal birth, it's crucial to aim for a healthy pregnancy, and try to eat clean 90% of the time.

Besides genetics, the amount of glucose available in the female body during gestation will affect her baby's growth. That's why, dear pregnant ladies, don't get too fat. Women who weigh more tend to have higher levels of blood sugar, and consequently bigger babies. Besides that, it might be quite impossible to 'naturally' go back to your original bodyweight if you overdo it.

Pregnancy is one of the few times in our lives when it's perfectly acceptable to gain weight. But, if you have no health issues, a nice fiber- and vitamin-rich diet should be more than enough for you and the baby growing inside your womb. Eating for two is a really bad idea.

And even if you pay a lot of attention to your nutrition, and you drink enough water so you don't overeat, you should always be aware that your body will NEVER be exactly the same after having a baby. Okay, maybe if your newborn weighs under 2.8 kilograms, you never breastfeed, and you manage to sleep your nights, maybe only then you can look and feel almost like before being pregnant. It's up to you, it's your body, it's your baby, and it's your choice. Every woman knows exactly what her priorities are. Nevertheless, keep in mind that your body is unique and may respond differently to the effects of pregnancy.

I am me and you are you, we are different, our metabolisms, food preferences and genetics are different, and our bodies will recover in different ways and at different speeds. Let's be realistic here! Not everyone has large breasts, wide hips, and a small waist. And, especially after having a baby, your body will suffer some big changes that will require adequate and consistent nutrition to support your healing, your mental health and emotional wellness.

My case: I am tall, skinny and my hips are narrow. I only gained 10 kilograms during both pregnancies but my belly was huge, and my babies were both big. And even if I managed to bounce back really quick to my pre-baby weight, my body will never look the same due to my poor skin elasticity, and because of my extremely obvious diastasis recti that still causes me discomfort and pain. Pregnancy puts so much pressure on the belly and sometimes the muscles just can't keep their shape, no matter how fit you are. Abdominal muscles don't always snap back into place weeks after delivery, and the chances are that you'll be stuck with your 'mommy tummy' forever, if you're carrying one or more big babies inside your belly, just like it happened to me.

Diastasis recti, or the splitting of your abdominal area, will result in a tummy pooch that can be unflattering, and, in some cases, dangerous. Don't underestimate it, as it might ruin your self-esteem even more than social media. And be aware that diastasis recti can go hand in hand with an umbilical hernia.

I'm still nostalgic about my beautiful innie ex-bellybutton. I remember watching it slowly go out during my first pregnancy. I knew that it would never go back to its original shape because it kind of turned inside out. And I was right. After my second pregnancy, my bellybutton was completely gone. An umbilical hernia repair could make it look 'normal' again, but people who decide to undergo this procedure must avoid anything that causes an increase in intra-abdominal pressure for at least six weeks after the intervention. Good luck with that, when you have young and energetic kids like mine!

It's important to know what your body needs and know its limitations. Don't compare your postpartum look to anyone else's. You have your own, one-of-a-kind body, you've been through a lot, and your pregnancy and birth experiences were most likely different from those of other women. So try ignoring all the 'perfect' pictures of celebrities on social media. They have ridiculous postpartum body standards, and it usually involves surgery. They are rich, have big houses with gardens, pools and home gyms, a lot of nannies, housekeepers, trainers and chefs who help them 24/7!

You've just created life and you don't have to put so much pressure on yourself. Instead of hating your body, do yourself a favor and focus on sleeping as much as you can, eat clean, and exercise regularly, even if it's just 5 minutes/day. You can always become a better version of yourself but you can't change the shape of your body, at least not without plastic surgery. So, unless you are ready to let a doctor 'fix' you, you'd better start loving your mirror again!

✳✳✳✳

When it comes to creating life there are some 'hidden issues', which nobody likes to mention, besides genetics. We hear very little about all these problems and yet they are affecting more than 40% of us.

Two of the most horrifying conditions I am referring to are urinary incontinence and fecal incontinence. A lot of women are dealing with the embarrassment caused by the involuntary leaking of urine or stool (or maybe only flatus, if you're lucky enough...) and Kegel don't solve the problem. These conditions are frequently associated with pregnancy and delivery, and their prevalence is totally underestimated.

There are studies which show that the proportion of women with fecal incontinence symptoms after a vaginal delivery is higher than that of women who had their baby delivered via C-section. The number of patients with urinary incontinence after a vaginal delivery is almost double compared to patients who went through a C-section. Nevertheless, there are also studies that demonstrated that all pregnant women can be affected by those horrifying conditions, and that a C-section delivery has no protective effect against fecal incontinence. The actual risk factors in all the studies are birth weight, duration of labor and pushing, and all the types of assisted vaginal deliveries, including the practice of episiotomy. Urinary incontinence can also be a symptom of pelvic organ prolapse, a really scary postpartum condition. It means that one of the following organs – uterus, vagina, bladder, rectum or small intestine –

would drop down from its position and would push against the vaginal walls, bulging into the vagina opening. Theoretically this condition is not so harmful, but without treatment it can get worse over time, leading to surgery almost always. Many doctors will recommend managing your weight through diet and exercise, since extra weight can put pressure on the pelvic floor, potentially causing damage. While Kegel exercises won't always improve symptoms, they can keep them from getting worse.

For those out there suffering in silence, don't be afraid. A prolapse is not life threatening. It is life altering, but you can learn to live with it. And if you don't like the answers you are getting from your current doctor, keep looking until you find someone with whom you feel comfortable, who really has your back, and who genuinely cares.

Did you know that more than 25% of all women will develop incontinence and/or pelvic organ prolapse as a result of vaginal childbirth? Do you know why? It's because we don't take postpartum recovery seriously!

Very few women receive quality postpartum care. Everyone expects them to fully recover after just six weeks, and to start having sex again! WTF people? Why is no one talking openly about postpartum rehabilitation? Why do we prefer going through surgery instead of preventing these issues? Why aren't all healthcare professionals prescribing postpartum therapy?

Apparently, France is one of the few European countries helping women to get back in shape, down there, after delivering a baby. They offer a very complex program called 'rééducation périnéale', which combines manual therapy, electrostimulation, and biofeedback. Its purpose is toning those fragile muscles surrounding the vagina and anus, so that every new mother can stay healthy and sexually satisfied, with no incontinence or pelvic pain whatsoever. 'La rééducation périnéale' is followed by 'la rééducation abdominale post-natale', which helps women strengthen their abdominal muscles, close their diastasis, and flatten their tummy through kinesiotherapy, massage, special breathing techniques and exercises. French doctors understand the importance of postpartum care, and everyone should learn from them!

❃❃❃❃

For some of us, the transformation our bodies go through, during and after pregnancy and vaginal birth, can be overwhelming. I think it's important to be mentally prepared for the 'new' you, and to be familiar with all the common postpartum problems. It's not easy, and it implies going beyond your comfort zone every single day. But, keep in mind that your body undergoes some serious changes to accommodate and birth your little bundle of joy, and those changes might take years to undo. We're talking about experiencing some scary heroic shit. First of all, besides all the tearing and scarring involved in the process of creating life, your postpartum vulva might be a totally different color than before, and second, your vagina will NEVER go back 100% to its original shape, no matter what they tell you.

You can make the tampon test. If it feels like your tampon is one sneeze away from sliding out, if it just doesn't stay inside like it used to before having kids, or if it feels painful and uncomfortable, if you need to insert it deeper and angle it in differently, if your tampon doesn't do the trick anymore and it leaks within an hour, or if you need to use a bigger one because the opening to your vagina is larger, it means you are different down there. Mega frustrating, I know... In any case, if you're not a fan of vaginal weights, or tightening creams, the only non-surgical solution to shrink your 'birth cannon' is to strengthen up that pelvic floor with some Kegels, regularly. However, don't expect miracles!

Dear doctors and midwives, please, stop tricking us into thinking that our bodies were designed to deliver babies vaginally. Stop hiding the realities of childbirth, and start talking about those shitty changes (physical and mental) that can affect one's body after vaginal delivery.

Yes, women have different birth experiences, and it's hard to predict if a delivery will be complicated or not. However, our lives would be easier if we would be prepared for the real postpartum issues.

Ladies, let's stop lying to ourselves! Why is childbirth still such a freaking taboo? And why does everybody want to hear only the 'good' stories? Why do we allow medical professionals to violate our bodies, and our minds? And why do they behave like they were set out to torment and kill us? We should ask more questions! And we should receive more apologies!

The TRUTH: vaginal birth can damage your body forever, and the probability that your genitalia will look and feel different post-delivery is very high. Ok, I suppose you won't care too much about this, but what about the fact that your sexual life will never be the same? Are you ready to feel discomfort during physical intimacy for the rest of your life? You might also have to 'do things' to your perineum in order to be able to poop properly. And this might turn you into a sad, frustrated, anxious woman, who is too embarrassed to tell anyone about her problems.

What I'm trying to say here is that vaginal birth also comes with RISKS. And the damage can be long-term and irreparable. I don't want you to assume that my C-section experience was better. It wasn't. But, please, don't be naïve! Instead, be aware that a vaginal delivery gone bad could have more negative effects on your body than a C-section. Pelvic injuries might be invisible to others, but they will decrease your quality of life. You might condemn yourself to suffering for a long, long time.

It's a shame that we still cannot talk openly about all this stuff. I think it would be very liberating to be able to share our birth stories with friends, during breakfast, or girls' night out. We rather try to hide our experiences, we feel ashamed, we avoid talking about our sexual life after childbirth, and choose not to admit that one in three women suffers in silence and never actually heals after going through birth trauma.

Most gynecologists will not acknowledge and treat physical damage caused by vaginal delivery, even if that's practically their job. That's why you should try to educate yourself before getting pregnant, so you won't feel miserable for the rest of your life. And, as I already mentioned earlier: bear in mind that your lady parts will never be the same after a vaginal delivery! Don't fool yourself, and don't let social media fool you. It's better to prepare for your new look instead of being sad about it.

As mentioned before, your sex life will also encounter new challenges, and you might experience a significant dip in sexual desire. Get ready for fake orgasms, less erotically fulfillment, and less enjoyable intercourse.

My case: I used to love my muff. Sex was such a joy, such a relaxation. I felt happy and creative after every orgasm. But, because I chose to put my trust in the German medical system, after a series of unfortunate events, my vulva looks like an exploded meatloaf, like a gathering of tongues that come in all different shapes and sizes, like it has been through mutilation and war. The only feeling I currently have towards both my vagina and vulva is pity. So, please, tell me how am I supposed to play with it? And how can I enjoy putting a penis (or a dildo) inside it when it looks and feels like a dying creature? No more 69s for me! My perineum is all gone, and my vagina leaks so much fluid sometimes that it goes right through my pants. It's so embarrassing...

After going through an overwhelming birth experience, twice, it took me years to be able to enjoy sex again. In the months following my C-section, my brain was extremely terrified, so it completely stopped any desire of unprotected coitus. Using condoms did not offer me enough safety, and I just couldn't put any medical tools inside my mutilated reproductive system. I didn't want to be touched or kissed, and I was ready to give up intimacy forever if there was even a very small chance that I could get pregnant again. So, basically, our sex life was put on hold until one day in June, when it became obvious that it was going to be: no vasectomy, no sex. However, my husband's vasectomy wasn't bad at all. It was performed under local anesthesia. He was awake for the procedure, didn't take any pain meds and forgot to use an ice pack afterwards.

✺✺✺✺

Having a baby is a deep, life-changing experience and most couples want to go through it together. Your partner can be an immensely reassuring presence to you in the delivery room. They need to see and feel everything, so they can understand and appreciate your hard work. It's a must, especially if you have a young, immature, selfish, and childish partner. Don't forget to bring some energy drinks with you, in case they decide to steal the show, and faint while you are in labor.

As for you, dear daddy-to-be, don't just go there and be useless, like a piece of furniture. You're not going to change the world by being scared and passive. Don't be a spectator. Instead, try to be present, and don't forget to praise your amazing partner. After all, she's the one who made it all possible. She's the one bringing your baby into this world. So be there, be supportive, be useful, and tell her how much you love her, and how much you appreciate what she's doing. Be her rock while her perineum is tearing like never before, and don't ever tell her to lower her voice, like my idiot husband did (shame on you, and on your selfish mother, who didn't raise you right!). It's absolutely ok to scream during labor, and it really helps. Becoming a parent often puts a strain on relationships, because it's much harder to be spontaneous and spend quality time together. So don't be surprised if you're not happy. Love is necessary, but love it's not enough. And sometimes you might feel that your relationship is no longer working, that you're miserable, and the love is gone.

Having a baby is one of the most life-changing events you'll ever experience. It's not all honey and roses, of course. But, if you want to be satisfied with what you have, you must embrace the changes, stop missing your past, and start redefining your love life. Be patient, as it might take more than a couple of months to be able to enjoy any kind of activity around your 'exploded' vagina.

Today, a couple of years after my C-section, and several years after my vaginal delivery, I can honestly say I'm very happy I don't have to go through childbirth ever again. I've eventually learned to accept the negative feelings and facts surrounding my two deliveries. Talking and writing about my problems helped me take control over my emotions again. It was a painful road, but I've grown through it. No more self-hatred and no more suicidal thoughts.

My first birth experience was filled with disappointment, and those terrifying images linger on and continue to disturb my mind sometimes, like fragments of a nightmare. Even now, years after having my daughter, I can't enjoy celebrating her birthday. As mentioned before, I delivered her vaginally, twenty-five hours after my water broke. When she came out of me, she was blue, couldn't breath, and needed maneuvers to be able to survive. I remember holding her and feeling utterly broken and shocked about what had just happened. During the first months of her life she had a lot of skin problems, probably because of all the drugs she involuntarily got from me during labor. Her tiny body was covered in spots and rashes, and she was visibly affected by it. (The only thing that really helped was applying breast milk to the affected areas) I felt so guilty. I couldn't stop crying for weeks. I kept telling myself that I was lucky we were both healthy. Physically I was broken, sore all over, and exhausted. My genitals hurt like hell, and I never received proper care post-delivery. I was literally falling apart when I first began to resent all doctors and midwives for torturing me, my daughter for damaging my body, my husband for a million reasons, big and small, and all mothers for not sharing the truth. I've tried, and I am still trying, to put this story, painful as it is, behind me. But, honestly, it still bothers me, both physically and mentally.

As you already know, I didn't get a chance to 'fix' my lady parts during my second delivery, as I had to go through an imposed, medically necessary, and unavoidable C-section. Our son got stuck in a breech position and we didn't manage to turn him no matter what we tried - acupuncture, moxibustion, chiropractic techniques, external cephalic version - nothing worked. So, eventually, I had to undergo surgery, a couple of days after everything failed. I was very sad about that turn of events. I felt mutilated, and I needed a lot of support from my husband to be able to feel normal again.

Two different pregnancies, two different birth experiences, two different babies... However, there is one big issue: my bond with our son is way stronger than the one I have with our daughter, even if I love them both enormously. With our daughter, I had to learn how to love, and how to grow as a mother. On the other hand, unconditional love came naturally with our son.

✵✵✵✵

In my opinion, it could be very helpful to know how many kids you want to have, before actually getting pregnant for the first time.

In my case, I knew from the beginning I wanted to have two kids. But I wasn't aware of the possible complications, like our son's breech position, that could easily lead to a C-section. I was completely uneducated on how natural birth occurs, even after reading a lot about it.

The sad reality is that very few women experience a true natural birth, and, in many cases, the ones to blame are the doctors and midwives who encourage the use of different induction methods without any medical reason. It's like an epidemic that destroys lives, and, even if healthcare professionals know about it, they don't care enough to stop it.

Their lack of compassion and kindness while working with pregnant women, as well as their crappy way of handling things during delivery, contribute to the surge of maternal birth-trauma and PTSD.

According to the Deutsche Gesellschaft für Psychosomatische Medizin und Psychotherapie, more than 4% of new mothers in Germany suffer from postpartum PTSD. And I am one of them. I was over half way into my second pregnancy when I realized that I won't survive without professional help. I reached out to my husband, and then asked my obstetrician about it, but it felt like I was talking to a wall.

Luckily, I later met an empathetic and wise therapist, who diagnosed me with trauma and post-traumatic stress, as a result of the physical and emotional ordeal of our daughter's birth.

Unfortunately, this is still a taboo topic, it carries a stigma, and it's not openly discussed. Women should be able to share their stories, and know that they will be listened to, cared for, and at least in some way, understood. So, why does our society remain indifferent towards our own rights and health, while millions of mothers are suffering in silence?

Know your rights or you will be mistreated during childbirth! It's important to analyze your situation and decide if you are ready to get cut 'everywhere' before it's too late. We all go through trauma in this life but not everyone is able to heal from it. However, our trauma doesn't have to define us. As Carl Jung said, 'I am not what has happened to me. I am what I choose to become.'

✳✳✳✳

Now, let's talk a bit about our post-baby breasts shall we? After all, they also deserve some attention and appreciation, since they are the fountains of milk, the source of that simple, yet so precious, cocktail of life.

Hormonal fluctuations, pregnancy, and breastfeeding, can lead to changes in the breast tissue. And, even if some studies suggest that breastfeeding does not increase breast sagging and asymmetries, I think it depends a lot on the body and genetic structure of each person. Many women request breast augmentation (or reduction) surgery after having a baby.

My case: Pumping milk ruined my breasts and nipples forever. Besides that, our beloved son decided to drink more from one side, which lead to a rather annoying new reality for me – different size boobs. My left boob is currently probably two sizes larger than my right one. And I must confess this problem makes me feel totally insecure, especially when I have to wear a swimsuit. Unfortunately, this kind of noticeable breast asymmetry can only be adjusted through surgery, and that's not an option for me. On top of that, my rib cage kind of expanded, and my bra size went down because of the weird transformation my body went through, while trying to accommodate babies inside. Normally, if you are lucky, your cup size will go and stay up, but it's wise to be prepared for the opposite situation as well. I don't regret breastfeeding our kids, but I cannot believe how deflated my breasts are.

Maybe it's not fair to say this, but I'm convinced that mothers who never breastfeed their babies are not properly connected to them, at least not through the real mother-baby connection. And a deficient bonding between mother and infant could have negative lifelong implications.

After giving birth, you will probably feel more or less lost in the mist of events. However, you should try to find your way out of the darkness and breastfeed your baby. It's such a magical experience. And, even when it feels like a very complicated and extremely stressful process, don't give up, and rest assured that your breasts are 100% perfect for your baby. Your brain is the one who freaks out.

And if you're not one of those lucky mommies who manage to breastfeed their newborn without any help, immediately after delivery, don't feel guilty. It will get better, just give it time.

Nevertheless, be aware that breastfeeding full-time can lead to chronic sleep deprivation, so ask your family to help you create a proper environment until you get used to it.

My case: after our daughter was born, I struggled a lot with breastfeeding guilt. Being surrounded by all those strong German new moms, who were able to breastfeed their babies within an hour of birth while my own breast didn't function, made me feel like a failure. Yes, it can be terrifying, and I still can't find my words to describe how disappointed I was back then. Fortunately, there are some things you can do to help yourself be great at breastfeeding, and reduce your stress levels postpartum.

1. Find yourself an experienced doula. Pick an older one. No offense, but they know more about breastfeeding than their younger colleagues, and you will really need both their knowledge, and their confidence to use that knowledge. Go to a quiet room, just you, your baby and your doula. Nobody else! No husband, no doctors, no strangers. Your home would

be the ideal place, but if you need to stay longer in hospital, any empty room will do the trick.

2. Hold your baby near your naked breasts, breath slowly, and try to relax. Listen to some calming music if you feel too nervous. Find a comfortable position and help your baby latch on to one of your nipples. It will hurt a bit, but don't be scared. Ask for help if you feel you can't properly do it. Your doula should be able to give you some helpful tips, without making a big fuss about it. Remember, nobody has the right to put pressure on you!

3. Keep your baby to yourself! During her first days on Earth she/he will need you more than ever. And you will also need those intimate moments. That closeness will make you more attuned to her needs, and will help create the bonding between the two of you. Consider co-sleeping. It can bring a lot of benefits. Besides making breastfeeding easier, sleeping close to your

baby will help her/him feel loved and secure; you might also sleep better, and feel more rested.

4. It's important to identify any problems, or signs of ineffective breastfeeding, as soon as possible. Last week, I stumbled upon a very emotional story about a baby who suffered brain damage after a couple of days of insufficient milk intake. After reading more about neonatal hypernatremia associated with lactation, I started questioning everything I know about breastfeeding. It's a very serious condition that can affect newborns, so, please, feed your baby properly. If you encounter breastfeeding difficulties, she/he might be at risk. That's why you should carefully monitor her/his weight during the first week of life. And stop comparing yourself to other women, everyone is unique, and it's not a competition. Breastfeeding is the best for your baby, but only if she/he is not starving in silence. You should not be ashamed if your body doesn't produce enough milk. Nor should

you feel superior to moms who can't breastfeed. Feeding your child correctly is the only essential thing. And being a good mother isn't just about your breast milk! Reading all the available information about breastfeeding can do you more harm than good sometimes. Try to prioritize true stories from real people, raw experiences of everyday mothers, because most books won't prepare you for the initial difficulties. The whole experience might not be what you've dreamed of, you might feel overwhelmed, alone and angry, and you might even decide to cease breastfeeding after a couple of days. And that's OK! Don't feel guilty about it because, after all, you are the best mom your baby could have, even if you can't control everything.

✹✹✹✹

Now, going back to the issues that affect women on their path to motherhood, I must warn you about some other pregnancy 'miracles'.

For instance, your shoe size might change. Your feet will for sure swell at some point, but they might as well stay bigger, forever! Your skin texture and pigmentation will also change, for better, or for worse. Discolorations, moles, stretch marks, spider veins, and acne, are nothing spectacular. Your nipples and the area around them will go darker because of the increase in hormones.

Postpartum hair loss is also a common problem, and sometimes it can take ages to regrow your hair, or worse, it may not grow back at all.

My case: my hair was thicker and shinier than ever while pregnant. Unfortunately, that didn't last after the babies were out, and I started losing a lot of hair, almost half of it. They say it's a common condition, caused by falling estrogen levels. But I must warn you, my hair never grew back to its original fullness. I guess the stress plays an important role, since it can soar to extreme levels sometimes.

As a woman and mother to be, it's extremely important to understand that the challenges one faces during pregnancy will contribute to the degradation of one's mental health postpartum. Being pregnant is not all 'glowing' and 'blooming'. It might be a special time, but it can also feel overwhelming and exhausting. And even if they say that the true knowledge of giving birth lies inside us women, our inner balance can still be ruined by various external factors. So, let's wake up, and make having babies an easier and more bearable experience.

1. Start by surrounding yourself with a bunch of caring people, who accept and appreciate you as you are, and whom you can trust in any situation.

2. Visit some hospitals (birth centers) and choose the one that feels right for you and your family. Don't just go to the nearest/biggest hospital. It will feel like a very cold and strange place, and they might not allow you to do what you want, or need, during labor. Even normal actions

such as walking, sitting, or drinking might be out of your control. So, open your eyes, and create your own path.

3. Labor and birth might be unpredictable and largely out of one's control because we can't plan for the unexpected. But, making a birth-plan, and trying to stick to it, might reduce the pressure put on women to give birth the 'right' way.

4. Nothing can guarantee a perfect birth outcome regardless of where it takes place. But, if you are a healthy and happy person, don't let doctors and midwives control your body and ruin it. If not medically needed, don't allow them to induce your labor. It blows up everything. The pain will be abnormal and unbearable, and the natural experience will be destroyed.

5. If you have a good doula (and enough courage) you could try giving birth at home. Imagine being able to labor inside your own private space, surrounded only by familiar faces. And then, when your baby is finally born, having the opportunity to use your own toilet and shower, and

sleep in your own bed. Imagine those moments of peace and quiet, with no nurses running around the room. It might sound unbelievable, but it's actually doable.

6. No matter what your future plans are, try to rest as much as possible during the last pregnancy weeks. Sleeping and relaxing before giving birth are decisive for your mental wellness, and, if you're expecting your first baby, you have no excuses. It's the perfect time to be selfish and think only about you, and your unborn child. All the other people and things can wait! After you give birth, you'll be a full-time mother, thrown way off balance, left with no time for yourself. If you're not able to find a comfortable position in your bed, try using pillows, sleep on the couch, take power naps on your desk during the day, do whatever it takes to sleep at least five hours every night.

7. If you want your parents around, now is the perfect time to ask them to come see

you. They should visit, but only if they are able to stop being arrogant, and if they are willing to help you relax. Let them cook for you, clean the house, spoil you, and help you pack some energy before giving birth.

My case: I felt extremely disappointed by my family's lack of empathy, and their exaggerated sense of self-importance. Shame on you mom, for being so selfish, and for baking cakes instead of talking to me about all that important stuff that could have saved me so many tears and unnecessary suffering. When I confronted you about your behavior, you told me you didn't realize you were supposed to help me, and that I should have let you know exactly what I needed. Silly me, always expecting people to do what I would do for them if they were in my shoes...

8. Giving birth can be a positive experience if both mom and baby come out healthy, and if (and only if) the woman feels respected and empowered the whole time during delivery. You should always trust

your gut! I'm not kidding, I realize this is the most common advice someone could give you, but, honestly, if I would have followed my intuition, I would have never given birth in Germany. I know there are countless places that are worse, when it comes to medical care, but there are undoubtedly quite a few places that are better. For instance, medical assistance services in any other language than German might be very hard to find. Doctors would rather speak their native language, and you can't complain about it. It's their country, you're the guest. If you're an expat, be sure to learn the local language (your partner should also be able to use it), or go back home to give birth, in an environment you will be more comfortable with.

9. If you do decide to give birth in Germany, get a better health insurance, which includes a private room just for you and your family. You won't have the option to pay for a private room later on, and it's nice not to have to share a

bathroom when you are bleeding like hell. Also, be aware that with public health insurance you can't choose neither the doctor, nor the methods and pain relievers used while in labor and during delivery. My case: my first German-hospital-experience as a public insured patient was a shock. Most employees were lazy, unfriendly, and sometimes even rude. There was a total lack of privacy, no respect whatsoever for the patients, and no specific rules for visitors. Nevertheless, I think that medical care standards may have a lot to do with luck (which hospital you choose, or the area you live in). During my first delivery, advice was almost always forced on me, and the birth process was totally medicalized. THEY were in charge, and they didn't offer any help with breastfeeding. There were always comments regarding vaginal birth versus C-section, especially about the costs implied for the German medical system. Nobody really cared about the patient, and nobody tried to explain the details. It was all about the costs, and about the ability to go through pain 'like a German', without showing feelings.

'Lady! You've got a healthy baby so why don't you stop complaining!' said the penis in the room.

As I mentioned before, when we moved to Germany we were given two options to choose from: the public and the private health insurance. We went for the public one because we were told that the private system does not offer better services, even if its costs are much higher. But, after going through some really hardcore shit, I would recommend anyone to get at least an extra coverage option on top of the public insurance, or, if financially possible, to switch to the private health insurance before having kids.

10. Maternity leave, however, is excellent in Germany because it's flexible. After the six weeks before, and eight after giving birth (which are paid 100%), a woman can apply for Elternzeit and Elterngeld, and

receive 65% of her previous salary for another 12 months. On top of that, every mother has the right to stay home with her baby for up to three years. The conditions are very generous compared to other European countries. So why do some of us see it as a sacrifice?

Why do you enjoy your job more than spending time with your family? You wanted the baby so much, why do you consider her/him a burden? Your job won't change, your baby will. And you'll miss that precious first year, all those big milestones. Just think about it, is it really worth it? I'm not saying you should give up your career and be a stay at home mother. I just want you to try and spend more than just a couple of months with your newborn because they grow so fast and, one day, you'll regret not being there.

❋❋❋❋

In both my pregnancies, my body acted on its own and, after a while, it just stopped 'talking' to me, and it felt no longer mine. I never enjoyed being pregnant, carrying my big belly here and there, and being constantly exhausted. To be honest, it felt like a very long hangover. Don't get me wrong, I love my children to the moon and back, but I totally don't miss being pregnant!

As you already know, with our daughter, things slowly began to spin out of my control, and I ended up going through a very brutal vaginal birth. With our son, the C-section wasn't nearly as traumatic as I anticipated, and the recovery was actually easier, painful and progressive, just like any recovery from abdominal surgery.

To all elective C-section moms: please stop hyperbolizing your pain! Any man could undergo a C-section if they had a uterus. It's a surgery and the baby is delivered by the medical personnel, while the lower part of your body is numb, and you cannot feel any pain. Stop comparing it with labor pain!

Giving birth vaginally is something that only certain women can do. It means you are going to be stretched out of your comfort zone and feel real pain while delivering your baby. It's extremely hard work. However, since I only experienced unnatural births, I'm not sure what would be the best option, if you want to deliver a drug-free, healthy baby.

Could it be a very long and chemically induced labor, followed by a traumatizing vaginal birth, where both mother and baby are stuffed with drugs, sometimes for more than 24 hours? Nope, that's not it! Been there, done that...

Or maybe an emergency C-section, after going through an agonizing labor and realizing it would never happen 'naturally'? Nope, that's not it either.

What about the Lamaze method, or maybe the Hypnobirthing method? I couldn't really say because I've never tried them. BUT, if I could turn back time, I would for sure try any natural strategy that might help calm down my anxiety and lead me towards a better birth experience. Nature is not perfect, but, when it comes to giving birth to a healthy baby, no one should recommend the induction of labor if there are no serious medical indications to do so. If we allow the natural progression of labor to happen, even if it takes longer, our bodies are able to adjust to the intensity of contractions over time, making the whole process bearable. You need to listen to your body, understand its signals. Nobody knows what you're going through better than you, and there might be times during your labor when you might feel like you need to do something different. Find the courage to say it loud because no one can get inside your brain. You are the expert on your body, and only you can interpret its signs.

You should also understand that not all women can safely deliver a baby vaginally. I'm not a birthing expert, I just write about my personal experience: one induced vaginal delivery and one medically necessary C-section. However, I did talk to different mothers, who had the chance to experience both natural and induced labor, and I believe that natural labor should always be prioritized. I'm not saying it's not painful, but when labor starts on its own, the pain will grow gradually, allowing your body to adapt. On the other hand, inducing labor can cause an incredible amount of abnormal pain that will for sure lead to the use of drugs.

I've also talked to some elective-C-section-mothers but, I must say, I can't really bond with them. I am biased and I tend to judge women by their birth stories. I didn't do it before experiencing birth myself.

I once met a young lady (let's call her Lily) who told me that, for her, giving birth and raising a baby was significantly easier than expected. At first, I thought she was joking, but after she realized I didn't believe her, she told me her story. Lily delivered her daughter via elective C-section on November 11, at 11am. She is still very proud that she got to choose the date herself. Because she didn't have time to go through labor, and since she wanted to keep her lady parts intact, in case she will have to get married again, Lily opted for a planned surgery. The Oberärztin tried to convince her to at least try going through labor, but she was not open to suggestions. She also decided that she wouldn't breastfeed her baby. Five days post-delivery, after coming home from the hospital, her daughter was left to sleep alone in her bed, and her husband was in charge of the feeding. So Lily kept on getting plenty of quality sleep. When I met her, six months after her elective C-section, she looked very fresh and sexy, a real stress-free mom. She is already planning for baby-number-two because her life is so easy and perfect.

Ella, another planned C-section mom, decided to intentionally have a big baby (4.2 kilograms) because she didn't want to be judged by her family and female friends for not going through labor. She gained 30 kilograms during her pregnancy, but after giving birth, she began to struggle with excess weight, and developed thyroid issues. Nevertheless, she is very happy that her vagina is intact.

My opinion: giving birth is a very complicated and bloody process. Keep in mind that, in some cases, a vaginal birth might be more complex than a C-section. If something goes wrong, you might end up with more than one surgery. Doctors will almost never understand the idea of 'natural' birth. Ok, maybe only female gynecologists, who gave birth vaginally themselves. But most of them will try to manage your birth, make it faster and easier for them, not for you.

Hospitals are scary places, and it's very difficult not to feel vulnerable when you're surrounded by strangers telling you what to do. Doctors and nurses are not superior human beings, as they like to believe. They can be very wrong sometimes, but they will never admit they made a mistake because the stakes for errors are high, and the hospital reputation may suffer. Besides this, they don't want to have to pay families for their mistakes. That's why, it's not unusual for errors to be kept secret by modifying records, or reflect events in a more favorable light than what actually happened. Unless infants have suffered permanent injuries, lawyers very rarely take on obstetric violence cases (which may claim malpractice, medical negligence, battery, and even fraud).

Women around the world face widespread abuse during childbirth. However, obstetric violence remains largely undocumented and unspoken about. New mothers themselves are not always aware that their experiences can be counted as abuse, and they are often shut down verbally when they cry out in pain.

Birth is a very fundamental experience for mothers. They need to be listened to, not shouted at, or subjected to brutal intimate torture. Remember that knowing your rights might save your life!

✳✳✳✳

Years after giving birth to my two children, I am finally ready to say it out loud: parenting is absolutely not how I thought it would be! I was slammed with the heaviness of my reality, and forced to embrace my new normal. Before being a mother, parenting looked like a natural process, a challenging, but rewarding affair. I was so naïve...

Having kids initially pushed me into the darkest corner of my mind. The huge responsibility of being a mother forced me to deny my authentic self, and it eventually killed my old identity. Being tired beyond what is healthy can really break you in pieces. Unfortunately, nobody really cares about sleep after having a baby. And nobody cares about the new mom. Biologically speaking, a woman's body should be ideally suited for having babies when she is in their twenties. But, her mind might be ready only twenty years later, when she had enough time to enjoy herself and her body, when she's truly ready to commit. What's the best age to have a baby? In my opinion, better later than too soon!

The first years in a mother's life are just a long period of sleep deprivation. There are no days off, food needs to be cooked, kids need to be taken care of, and relationship stability must not be ignored. And let's not forget about the stomach viruses, the puke on the carpets, and the diarrhea in the socks, the high fever, and all the worries that chase a mother on a daily basis. Anxiety, wrinkles, gray hair, and little Lego pieces all over the place, quietly waiting for you to step on them and suffer...

New mothers can be really lonely and feel isolated. So what do other mothers do to 'help' them? They make them feel ugly and fat, criticize their appearance and their abilities, bringing negativity into their life. Why do we care so much about what others think of us? Hmmm, I don't have an answer to that question, but honestly this subject (postpartum body-shaming) doesn't affect me anymore. I've learned to stop focusing on my outside body. Instead,

I started focusing on what my inside body NEEDS.

Whether it's hormonal, nutritional, or something else, like the fact that your baby is crying all the time and you barely sleep, just stop criticizing your own body. It's the only one you have! It's your HOME. So, take good care of it, make the changes you need to make, relax and take your time, even if we all know that being a mother generally means neglecting yourself, your health, and your own needs.

My case: having kids literally sucked the life out of my body, suppressed my immune system, and increased my everyday stress levels. I'm not joking. However, I do feel more mature than any childless lady out there. I also stopped giving a crap about what other people think about me, and I began making better decisions. I somehow managed to filter 'bad' people out of my life, by simply shutting my senses off to anything that isn't essential, or doesn't add value to my existence. Judgmental people, who think they are entitled to comment on somebody else's life, are everywhere. Learn to ignore them. Live your dreams, make your own choices, try to become immune to other people's poison, and remember that nothing will make you less of a mother.

Motherhood is hard as hell. You are not the old-you anymore, your body is not the same, you've changed and you must learn to love the new-you. You are super-mom, you are great at what you do, you're the caretaker, the chef, the provider, the one who plans and organizes everything for the family, keeping everyone healthy and happy. You certainly deserve a medal! Motherhood can be very demanding, but it's also extremely rewarding. Remember to enjoy it as much as you can, and don't get fooled by those pictures of mothers smiling all the time. That's rarely an accurate depiction of what's really going on inside their lives.

Being a parent is the most complex job on Earth. Keeping a child safe, help her/him survive as a teenager, throughout the age of sex and drugs (even if it's just alcohol and cigarettes), providing order and consistency, by setting limits and encouraging positive behavior, showing affection and infinite love, each of these actions require a lot of effort and self-sacrifice, and you will not be able to enjoy every moment.

As a parent, you will always try to do everything for your kids. And even if sometimes you will yell at them, and you'll feel a lot of relief when they go to bed, remember that that's ok, and that you're not a failure. And don't compare yourself to other parents! Your kids are unique, you are unique as well. Listen to your heart, be happy, love your kids just the way they are, make your own decisions, and stop caring about what others think of you. My case: taking care of our daughter for four years before delivering our son was an all-consuming task. Becoming a mother for the first time was by far the most overwhelming experience for me, and I only realized that after having a second baby. Everything went so much smoother with our son, even if he cried a lot more than his sister. It took me two kids to be able to enjoy motherhood. And believe me, no matter how many child development books you read, no matter how many stories you hear, your own experience is your true source of knowledge. The challenge of being a tired, scared, and even irritated (but never bored) parent gave a new meaning to my life.

I adore our two monkeys but, frankly, I couldn't imagine having more kids! Being a mother killed the funny part of my personality and turned me into an anxious, demanding, abundantly cautious, almost paranoid, but very creative, yet down-to-earth person. I might look a hundred years older than before, but I finally understand what true, unconditional love means. And, even if raising these two little persons into good humans is a lot of work, I wouldn't change a thing about them because having them in my life is just amazing.

There is no perfect parent, but you should try to act as a role model, even if you don't feel like it, because your kids are watching you carefully all the time, and will copy everything they see at home. Children are sometimes like a storm, they can bring out the worst in you and it can be difficult to calm your anger.

So, if you tend to get angry and yell, like I do, or if you're having a really bad day, and you feel bitter and frustrated, don't just throw it on them. You'll break their innocence into pieces and it's not worth it. Instead, take a break... focus your energy on something else, and breathe deeply before acting impulsively in front of your children. If you can understand what's triggering your anger, you can be more aware of your thoughts, and you can definitely find some techniques to react to stress more calmly.

Keep in mind that if you are violent towards others, your kids will also be.

✳✳✳✳

My dearest daughter,

Nothing compares to becoming a mother for the first time. And nothing and nobody can really prepare you for it. It is one of those things you won't be able to understand without experiencing it yourself, no matter what.
Being a mom is the most beautiful job in this entire world, but it's also the hardest. Walking the path of motherhood can be overwhelming. Be aware that nothing will be the same after having kids, starting with you. Your life will suddenly stop being important, and you might even have to give up your own dreams. But, if you are not afraid to go with your intuition, you'll be fine.
If YOU choose to give birth vaginally, understand that a 100% natural birth is just a beautiful dream. Don't be fooled by it like I was. And remember, there is no 'best birth' competition!
Breast milk might be the perfect food for your baby, but deciding whether or not to

breastfeed should be your own personal decision.

Be honest with yourself. You don't have to please everyone. It's impossible, so don't even bother trying.

And if you want to raise your kids into healthy, open-minded and creative adults, start with a clean nutrition, and make sure to spend enough quality time with them.

I love you and your brother more than words can describe. And, even if I might have acted like an overprotective fool sometimes, I want you to know how proud I am to be your mom. It's a privilege to watch you both grow. Your creativity and your inner beauty inspire me every day. Thank you for all the love you have been giving me!

Love,
Mom

I wrote this book as part of my healing therapy program, to keep my mind busy during a rough patch in my life. I only did it to stay sane, as it helped me control my darkest demons. And even if the process of writing it brought back those horrible nightmares, it also made them fade away and allowed me to sleep again, and enjoy life after a serious mental health crisis. It took me years to learn how to accept the changes my body and mind have been through, and it wasn't easy to love my new self. Writing about my experiences helped me understand and process my feelings. Yes, it might sound like a cliché, but it did comfort me more than talking to my psychotherapist.

© 2023, THE JUNGFRAU
Herstellung und Verlag: BoD – Books on Demand, Norderstedt
ISBN: 9783734717642